The Church Triumphant

Through the Book of Acts

By A.L. and Joyce Gill

ISBN 0-941975-35-5

Powerhouse Publishing
P.O. Box 99
Fawnskin, CA 92333
(909) 866-3119

Books by A.L. and Joyce Gill

God's Promises For Your Every Need
Destined For Dominion
Out! In The Name Of Jesus
Victory Over Deception

Study Guides in This Series

Authority Of The Believer
How To Quit Losing
and Start Winning

God's Provision For Healing
Receiving and Ministering
God's Healing Power

Ministry Gifts
Apostle, Prophet, Evangelist,
Pastor, Teacher

Miracle Evangelism
God's Plan to Reach the World

New Creation Image
Knowing Who You Are in Christ

Patterns For Living
From the Old Testament

Praise And Worship
Becoming Worshipers of God

Supernatural Living
Through the Gifts of the Holy Spirit

Acknowledgment
It is with great appreciation that we acknowledge
the contribution of Lin Rang for her many hours of work on the
***The Church Triumphant.** Her suggestions and additions to this work*
have contributed greatly to its completion.

About the Authors

A.L. and Joyce Gill are internationally known speakers, authors and Bible teachers. A.L.'s apostolic ministry travels have taken him to over fifty nations of the world, preaching to crowds exceeding one hundred thousand in person and to many millions by radio and television.

Their top-selling books and manuals have sold over two million copies in the United States. Their writings, which have been translated into many languages, are being used in Bible schools and seminars around the world.

The powerful life-changing truths of God's Word explode in the lives of others through their dynamic preaching, teaching, writing and video and audio tape ministry.

The awesome glory of the presence of God is experienced in their praise and worship seminars as believers discover how to become true and intimate worshipers of God. Many have discovered a new and exciting dimension of victory and boldness through their teachings on the authority of the believer.

The Gills have trained many believers to step into their own God-given supernatural ministries with the healing power of God flowing through their hands. Many have learned to be supernaturally natural as they are released to operate in all nine gifts of the Holy Spirit in their daily lives and ministries.

Both A.L. and Joyce have Master of Theological Studies degrees. A.L. has also earned a Doctor of Philosophy in Theology degree from Vision Christian University. Their ministry in solidly based on the Word of God, is centered on Jesus, strong in faith and taught in the power of the Holy Spirit.

Their ministry is a demonstration of the Father's heart of love. Their preaching and teaching are accompanied by powerful anointing, signs, wonders, and healing miracles with many being slain in waves under the power of God.

Signs of revival including waves of holy laughter, weeping before the Lord and awesome manifestations of God's glory and power are being experienced by many who attend their meetings.

A Word to Teachers and Students

Jesus announced, **I will build my church, and the gates of Hades shall not prevail against it.** This thrilling, topical study of the book of Acts reveals that church in action as a pattern for our lives and ministries today. It will inspire the student into a new and greater dimension of supernatural living as signs, wonders and miracles are released in their daily lives.

We suggest that before teaching this course you read through the the book of Acts several times, until it becomes alive in your spirit. It is also suggested that the teacher study the Epistles of the New Testament as they relate to the events, places, people and truths found in the book of Acts.

The more you saturate yourself with the truths, the lifestyle and the patterns of ministry from the book of Acts the more these truths will move from your mind into your spirit. This manual will then provide the outline for you to use as you impart these truths to others.

Personal life illustrations are a must for effective teaching. The author has omitted these from this work so that the teacher will provide illustrations from his or her own rich experiences, or those of others to which the students will be able to relate.

It should always be remembered that it is the Holy Spirit who has come to teach us all things, and that when we are studying or when we are teaching we should always be empowered and led by the Holy Spirit.

This study is excellent for personal or group studies, Bible schools, Sunday schools and home groups. It is important that both the teacher and the student have copies of this manual during the course of the study.

The best books are written in, underlined, meditated upon and digested. We have left space for your notes and comments. The format has been designed with a fast reference system for review and to assist you in finding areas again. The special format makes it possible for each person, once they have studied through this material, to teach the contents to others.

Paul wrote to Timothy:
And the things you have heard from me among many witnesses, commit these to faithful men who will be able to teach others also 2 Timothy 2:2

This course is designed as a practical participation Bible course in the MINDS (Ministry Development System) format which is a specially developed approach to programmed learning. This concept is designed for multiplication in the lives, the ministry and the future teaching of the students. Former students, by using this manual, can teach this course easily to others.

Table of Contents

Section One – Birth Of The Church

Lesson One	Beginnings of the Church	7
Lesson Two	Promise of Power	13
Lesson Three	Coming of the Holy Spirit	20
Lesson Four	Battle Over the Name of Jesus	25
Lesson Five	Jesus' Plan for the Church	33
Lesson Six	An Example for Today	45

Section Two – Ministries in the Book of Acts

Lesson Seven	Peter the Reed	53
Lesson Eight	Peter the Rock	62
Lesson Nine	To Die Is Gain	71
Lesson Ten	Philip the Evangelist	78
Lesson Eleven	Conversion of Saul	83
Lesson Twelve	Ministry and Death of Paul	90
Lesson Thirteen	We Are the Church Triumphant	102

SECTION ONE

BIRTH OF THE CHURCH

Lesson One

Beginnings of the Church

INTRODUCTION TO ACTS

The beginning of the church is found in the book of Acts, and so this course on the Church Triumphant is centered in the book of Acts. This book could be renamed the Acts of the Apostles Through the Power of the Holy Spirit or the Acts of the Holy Spirit Through the Apostles.

It is impossible to study the beginnings of the church, or the book of Acts without learning about the Holy Spirit.

The book of Acts should never be studied simply as history. It should be studied as a manual of God's plan and purpose for the church today.

For example, it is not as important to remember that Paul reached the people in Ephesus with the gospel of Jesus Christ as it is to understand that how Paul reached the people in Ephesus is a pattern for evangelism today.

God has not changed His patterns and methods. We are to reach those around us, and throughout the whole world in the same way as did the early disciples. The power that He gave to the early believers, He has given us today.

Two Sections

The book of Acts could be divided into two sections.

Chapters 1-12 Peter and his ministry

Peter was the apostle to the Jews.

Chapters 13-28 Paul and his ministry

Paul was the apostle to the Gentiles.

Major Ministries

There are several major ministries of the book of Acts which we will study as examples of how we are to minister today.

➢ Peter
➢ Stephen
➢ Philip
➢ Paul

BACKGROUND OF BOOK OF ACTS

Seven Major Churches

The seven major churches spoken about in the book of Acts were located mainly in the country we know today as Turkey. Outside of Turkey, there was the church in Jerusalem and in Antioch.

Luke the Author

The author of the book of Acts was Luke, a Greek doctor from Antioch. He was the only Gentile to write books in the New Testament. He wrote from a background of investigation, evidently by both reading and talking to those who had been with Jesus from the first. As far as we know he was the first church historian.

Luke 1:1-4 Inasmuch as many have taken in hand to set in order a narrative of those things which are most surely believed among us, just as those who from the beginning were eyewitnesses and ministers of the word delivered them to us, it seemed good to me also, having had perfect understanding of all things from the very first, to write to you an orderly account, most excellent Theophilus, that you may know the certainty of those things in which you were instructed.

Luke did not write about himself.

We know that he joined Paul in some of his travels. Luke wrote the book of Acts and when he was with Paul, he uses the term "we."

Acts 16:10 Now after he had seen the vision, immediately we sought to go to Macedonia, concluding that the Lord had called us to preach the gospel to them.

We know that Luke was a physician.

Colossians 4:14 Luke the beloved physician and Demas greet you.

At one time, Luke was the only one who remained with Paul. All of the others had deserted him.

2 Timothy 4:11a Only Luke is with me.

Date of Writing

The book of Acts was written about 63-65 AD, and covers thirty years of ministry.

This study is not a complete, comprehensive study of the book of Acts. It has as its center focus the beginning of the church and how it relates to us today.

FIRST MENTION OF THE CHURCH

The word, "church", was first mentioned in the Bible when Jesus was talking to his disciples at Caesarea Phillipi.

Matthew 16:18 And I also say to you that you are Peter, and on this rock I will build My church, and the gates of Hades shall not prevail against it.

Peter had just made the statement of faith, "Thou art Christ the Son of God." Then Jesus said that on the truth, the "Rock", He would build His church.

Jesus did not talk about an early church and later church. He mentioned only one church and He said two things about that church. The first was that He would build it – "I will build my church." The second was that the gates of Hades would not overcome that church.

The gates of Hades that Jesus spoke of referred to the governments of Satan. Jesus said that He would build His church and that Satan would not be able to overcome it!

The church that Jesus was to build was to be a powerful, overcoming victorious church.

Record of Church

The twenty-eight chapters of the book of Acts record many of the events of the church that Jesus was building showing the:

➤ Prominence of the Holy Spirit
➤ Power (dunamis) of the Holy Spirit
➤ Place of the Holy Spirit
➤ Purpose of the Holy Spirit: to enable believers to fulfill the Great Commission of Jesus.

Matthew 28:19 Go therefore and make disciples of all the nations, baptizing them in the name of the Father and of the Son and of the Holy Spirit ...

Mark 16:15 And He said to them, "Go into all the world and preach the gospel to every creature."

THE GREAT COMMISSION

Jesus did not instruct His disciples to do something that they could not do. Just before He left this earth, He gave them His last instructions. We refer to these instructions as the "Great Commission."

Mark 16:15,17,18 And He said to them, "Go into all the world and preach the gospel to every creature. And these signs will follow those who believe: in My name they will cast out demons; they will speak with new tongues; they will take up serpents; and if they drink anything deadly, it will by no means hurt them; they will lay hands on the sick, and they will recover."

Jesus instructed the believers to go to the whole world and tell them the good news. And then Jesus said that He would send signs with those who believed in His name to confirm His Word.

Mark 16:20 And they went out and preached everywhere, the Lord working with them and confirming the word through the accompanying signs. Amen.

God's plan has not changed. We are still to go into all the world and preach the gospel of Jesus Christ to every creature and to believe that in His name the same signs and wonders will follow.

The "Alls" of Victory!

Matthew 28:18-20 Then Jesus came and spoke to them, saying, "All authority has been given to Me in heaven and on earth. Go therefore and make disciples of all the nations, baptizing them in the name of the Father and of the Son and of the Holy Spirit, teaching them to observe all things that I have commanded you; and lo, I am with you always, even to the end of the age." Amen.

➢ Jesus has all authority.
➢ Through that authority we are to make disciples of all nations.
➢ We are to teach them all (everything) we have been taught.
➢ Jesus is with us always. He is with us anywhere He sends us on this earth. He is with us now and even to the very end of the age.
➢ And this is all so that we can take the gospel to every person on the face of this earth.

INTRODUCTION OF HOLY SPIRIT

If Jesus is going to build a powerful church, not defeated by Satan, it is important that we understand the patterns of the church's beginnings. It is crucial in understanding the development of the church to know why the Holy Spirit is in the world today.

The Counselor

Jesus said that it was important that He go away so that the Holy Spirit could come.

John 16:7-11 Nevertheless I tell you the truth. It is to your advantage that I go away; for if I do not go away, the Helper will not come to you; but if I depart, I will send Him to you.

The Convictor

And when He has come, He will convict the world of sin, and of righteousness, and of judgment: of sin, because they do not believe in Me; of righteousness, because I go to My Father and you see Me no more; of judgment, because the ruler of this world is judged.

Necessary in Our Lives

Jesus instructed us to wait until the power of the Holy Spirit came upon us so that we could be witnesses in our home town, the surrounding areas and then to the ends of the world.

Acts 1:4,5,8 And being assembled together with them, He commanded them not to depart from Jerusalem, but to wait for the Promise of the Father, "which," He said, "you have heard from Me; for John truly baptized with water, but you shall be baptized with the Holy Spirit not many days from now.

But you shall receive power when the Holy Spirit has come upon you; and you shall be witnesses to Me in Jerusalem, and in all Judea and Samaria, and to the end of the earth."

The Trinity Revealed

In the Old Testament, we learn about God the Father. Looking back from the advantage point of the New Testament, we see both the work of the Son and the Holy Spirit.

In the Gospels the Second Person of the triune God is revealed. We receive a revelation of the Son – Jesus.

Jesus revealed the Holy Spirit as the Third Person of the Trinity. A study of the book of Acts will bring us to an intimate knowledge of the Holy Spirit.

FUNCTIONS OF HOLY SPIRIT

Guide

John 16:13-15 However, when He, the Spirit of truth, has come, He will guide you into all truth; for He will not speak on His own authority, but whatever He hears He will speak; and He will tell you things to come.

Bring Glory to Jesus

He will glorify Me, for He will take of what is Mine and declare it to you. All things that the Father has are Mine. Therefore I said that He will take of Mine and declare it to you.

Instruct and Command

Acts 1:2 Until the day in which He was taken up, after He through the Holy Spirit had given commandments to the apostles whom He had chosen.

Acts 8:29 Then the Spirit said to Philip, "Go near and overtake this chariot."

Acts 10:19-21 While Peter thought about the vision, the Spirit said to him," Behold, three men are seeking you. Arise therefore, go down and go with them, doubting nothing; for I have sent them."

Then Peter went down to the men who had been sent to him from Cornelius, and said, "Yes, I am he whom you seek. For what reason have you come?"

Select and Reveal

Acts 13:2 As they ministered to the Lord and fasted, the Holy Spirit said, "Now separate to Me Barnabas and Saul for the work to which I have called them."

Strengthen and Encourage

Acts 9:31 Then the churches throughout all Judea, Galilee, and Samaria had peace and were edified. And walking in the fear of the Lord and in the comfort of the Holy Spirit, they were multiplied.

Give Power

➤ *To be Witnesses*

Acts 1:8 But you shall receive power when the Holy Spirit has come upon you; and you shall be witnesses to Me in Jerusalem, and in all Judea and Samaria, and to the end of the earth.

➤ *To Speak in Tongues*

Acts 2:4 And they were all filled with the Holy Spirit and began to speak with other tongues, as the Spirit gave them utterance.

➤ *To Have Dreams & Visions*

Acts 2:17 And it shall come to pass in the last days, says God, That I will pour out of My Spirit on all flesh; your sons and your daughters shall prophesy, your young men shall see visions, your old men shall dream dreams.

➤ *To Prophesy*

Acts 2:18 And on My menservants and on My maidservants I will pour out My Spirit in those days; and they shall prophesy.

QUESTIONS FOR REVIEW

1. What is the most important thing to learn in the book of Acts? How should it be studied?

2. What is the "Great Commission?" List as many aspects of it as you can.

3. Name at least three things the Holy Spirit does in the life of the believer.

Lesson Two

Promise of Power

WHAT POWER?

Jesus was empowered by the Holy Spirit and He promised His believers power.

John 16:7 Nevertheless I tell you the truth. It is to your advantage that I go away; for if I do not go away, the Helper will not come to you; but if I depart, I will send Him to you.

Acts 1:8 But you shall receive power when the Holy Spirit has come upon you; and you shall be witnesses to Me in Jerusalem, and in all Judea and Samaria, and to the end of the earth.

Source of Power

Jesus promised to send the same Holy Spirit that was the source of His power while He was on this earth.

Romans 8:11 But if the Spirit of Him who raised Jesus from the dead dwells in you, He who raised Christ from the dead will also give life to your mortal bodies through His Spirit who dwells in you.

With this same great power, Jesus promised that we as His believers would be able to do the same things that He had been doing.

John 14:12 Most assuredly, I say to you, he who believes in Me, the works that I do he will do also; and greater works than these he will do, because I go to My Father.

Overcoming Power

Every believer would become an important part of His church. As a part of His church every believer would need the victorious overcoming power of the Holy Spirit.

Matthew 16:18 And I also say to you that you are Peter, and on this rock I will build My church, and the gates of Hades shall not prevail against it.

Power of Holy Spirit

If we are to be as victorious in our lives as Jesus was in His life, we are not to try to live our lives in our own power. Instead, He told His disciples to wait until they had received the power of the Holy Spirit.

Acts 1:4 And being assembled together with them, He commanded them not to depart from Jerusalem, but to wait for the Promise of the Father, "which," He said, "you have heard from Me ...

Same Power

This was the same power of the Holy Spirit that Paul asked the Ephesian believers if they had received when, or since, they received Jesus as their Savior.

Acts 19:2,6 He said to them, "Did you receive the Holy Spirit when you believed?"

And they said to him, "We have not so much as heard whether there is a Holy Spirit."

And when Paul had laid hands on them, the Holy Spirit came upon them, and they spoke with tongues and prophesied.

Power for All

If Jesus and the early believers needed this power, even so, we as believers today, need the power of the Holy Spirit in our lives.

JESUS, OUR EXAMPLE

We must understand how the Holy Spirit worked through the life of Jesus to understand how He worked through the people of the New Testament and to know how He wants to work through us today.

Anointed by Holy Spirit

Acts 10:38 how God anointed Jesus of Nazareth with the Holy Spirit and with power, who went about doing good and healing all who were oppressed by the devil, for God was with Him.

Jesus is the example to believers in everything they are called upon to face. He is our example:

➢ As Teacher
➢ As Minister
➢ As Leader
➢ As the Good Shepherd
➢ As Healer
➢ As Ruler
➢ In water baptism
➢ In meeting temptation
➢ In personal relationships
➢ In setting priorities
➢ In personal witnessing
➢ In being under authority
➢ In facing persecution
➢ In dying
➢ In humility
➢ In compassion
➢ In love
➢ In righteousness anger

> In humor
> In sorrow

He is our example in every area of our lives as we too are anointed by the Holy Spirit.

> *To Preach & Heal*

Luke 4:18 The Spirit of the Lord is upon Me, because He has anointed Me to preach the gospel to the poor. He has sent Me to heal the brokenhearted, to preach deliverance to the captives and recovery of sight to the blind, to set at liberty those who are oppressed ...

As Jesus ministered in the power of the Holy Spirit, even so we today must minister in the power of the Holy Spirit. Jesus was an example to His disciples of one who ministered in that power. The disciples learned by what Jesus did before they learned by what He taught.

Acts 1:1 The former account I made, O Theophilus, of all that Jesus began both to do and teach.

Jesus was qualified to be our perfect example, because the works that He did on this earth He did as a man, and not as God. He was truly human, yet at the same time, He was still truly God.

Rights as God, Laid Aside

Philippians 2:5-7 Let this mind be in you which was also in Christ Jesus, Who, being in the form of God, did not consider it robbery to be equal with God, but made Himself of no reputation, taking the form of a servant, and coming in the likeness of men.

All authority, dominion and rule on earth had been given to man and woman when God created Adam and Eve. In all the universe, God retained His authority and rule. However, on earth, it had all been given to mankind.

Genesis 1:26,28 Then God said, "Let Us make man in Our image, according to Our likeness; let them have dominion over the fish of the sea, over the birds of the air, and over the cattle, over all the earth and over every creeping thing that creeps on the earth."

Then God blessed them, and God said to them, "Be fruitful and multiply; fill the earth and subdue it; have dominion over the fish of the sea, over the birds of the air, and over every living thing that moves on the earth."

If Jesus was to take this stolen authority away from Satan and restore it to man, He Himself must operate on this earth in authority as a man and not as God. For this reason and also in order to become our perfect substitute, He came to this earth as a man, the "last Adam."

> *Became Last Adam*
> *Is "Son of Man"*

1 Corinthians 15:45 And so it is written, "The first man Adam became a living being." The last Adam became a life-giving spirit.

Jesus' authority on this earth was because He was the "Son of Man."

John 5:25-27 Most assuredly, I say to you, the hour is coming, and now is, when the dead will hear the voice of the Son of God; and those who hear will live. For as the Father has life in Himself, so He has granted the Son to have life in Himself, and has given Him authority to execute judgment also, because He is the Son of Man.

As the "Son of Man," the "last Adam" and because He was truly a man who had laid aside His rights and privileges as God, Jesus became our perfect example. We notice that as a man, no miracles happened in the life of Jesus until He had received the power of the Holy Spirit. If Jesus, as our perfect example, needed the power of the Holy Spirit, we too need to receive the power of the Holy Spirit in our lives.

➤ *Did Nothing of Himself*

Jesus said that He could do nothing of Himself

John 5:19 Then Jesus answered and said to them, "Most assuredly, I say to you, the Son can do nothing of Himself, but what He sees the Father do; for whatever He does, the Son also does in like manner."

➤ *Anointed by Holy Spirit*

Jesus was anointed of the Holy Spirit to do the will of God.

Luke 4:18 The Spirit of the Lord is upon Me, because He has anointed Me to preach the gospel to the poor. He has sent Me to heal the brokenhearted, to preach deliverance to the captives and recovery of sight to the blind, to set at liberty those who are oppressed ...

Acts 10:38 ... how God anointed Jesus of Nazareth with the Holy Spirit and with power, who went about doing good and healing all who were oppressed by the devil, for God was with Him.

➤ *Holy Spirit – Miracle Worker*

Jesus does not have to be here physically for miraculous things to happen. The same Holy Spirit who empowered Jesus is here today to empower all believers.

John 14:12 Most assuredly, I say to you, he who believes in Me, the works that I do he will do also; and greater works than these he will do, because I go to My Father.

Jesus promised His believers that when He went to His Father, He would send the Holy Spirit. He also promised that when the Holy Spirit came upon them they would be His witnesses. They were to be His witnesses by doing what He had been doing in the power of the Holy Spirit.

Jesus Limited by Unbelief

Mark 6:1-5 Then He went out from there and came to His own country, and His disciples followed Him. And when the Sabbath had come, He began to teach in the synagogue.

And many hearing Him were astonished, saying, "Where did this Man get these things? And what wisdom is this which is given to Him, that such mighty works are performed by His hands! "Is this not the carpenter, the Son of Mary, and brother of James, Joses, Judas, and Simon? And are not His sisters here with us?" And they were offended at Him.

But Jesus said to them, "A prophet is not without honor except in his own country, among his own relatives, and in his own house." Now He could do no mighty work there, except that He laid His hands on a few sick people and healed them.

The great multitude was there and there were many that needed healings but Jesus healed only a few. Why was this?

It was because there were so many unbelievers. The Holy Spirit works by faith so the Holy Spirit led Him to the only man with faith ready to receive!

Many today have failed to do the works of Jesus and receive the healing power of Jesus because of lack of teaching and unbelief.

FIRST CHAPTER OF ACTS

First Promise

There are two promises in the first chapter of the book of Acts. The first was that the power of the Holy Spirit would come.

It is interesting that Luke started the book of Acts with the end of Jesus' time on this earth.

He had ended the book of Luke with the words of Jesus,

Luke 24:49 Behold, I send the Promise of My Father upon you; but tarry in the city of Jerusalem until you are endued with power from on high.

Now he begins the book of Acts with the same words.

Acts 1:4b-5 He commanded them not to depart from Jerusalem, but to wait for the Promise of the Father, "which," He said, "you have heard from Me; for John truly baptized with water, but you shall be baptized with the Holy Spirit not many days from now."

Then He continues;

Acts 1:8 "But you shall receive power when the Holy Spirit has come upon you; and you shall be witnesses to Me in Jerusalem, and in all Judea and Samaria, and to the end of the earth."

Second Promise

The second promise was of the return of Jesus to earth again. Through all ages of the church, believers have waited for, watched for and hoped for the return of Jesus to the earth.

Acts 1:10,11 And while they looked steadfastly toward heaven as He went up, behold, two men stood by them in white apparel, Who also said, "Men of Galilee, why do you stand gazing up into heaven? This same Jesus, who was taken up from you into heaven, will so come in like manner as you saw Him go into heaven."

In the same passage of scripture, we are given the promise of the power we need through the Holy Spirit to be victorious on this earth and the encouragement of looking for Jesus' return.

End of Judas

The subject of Judas was dealt with while the believers waited for the coming of the Holy Spirit. Peter talked of him and told how even his death was a fulfillment of prophecy.

Acts 1:20 For it is written in the book of Psalms: 'Let his habitation be desolate, and let no one live in it'; and, 'Let another take his office.'

The early church did not ignore sin, it was dealt with. The same should be true today. There was no need for discipline because Judas had judged himself.

Following that reading of David's prophecy they moved in obedience to the Word and selected another apostle to take the place of Judas. Since only God can select an apostle, they chose two and then prayed for the Lord to select the right one by the casting of lots.

Matthias Chosen

Acts 1:23-26 And they proposed two: Joseph called Barsabas, who was surnamed Justus, and Matthias.

And they prayed and said, "You, O Lord, who know the hearts of all, show which of these two You have chosen to take part in this ministry and apostleship from which Judas by transgression fell, that he might go to his own place." And they cast their lots, and the lot fell on Matthias. And he was numbered with the eleven apostles.

REASONS HOLY SPIRIT CAME

To Baptize

The Holy Spirit baptizes us into the body of Christ.

I Corinthians 12:13 For by one Spirit we were all baptized into one body—whether Jews or Greeks, whether slaves or free—and have all been made to drink into one Spirit.

To Indwell

He came to indwell every believer.

I Corinthians 6:19,20 Or do you not know that your body is the temple of the Holy Spirit who is in you, whom you have from God, and you are not your own? For you were bought at a price;

therefore glorify God in your body and in your spirit, which are God's.

To Empower

He came to empower believers.

Acts 1:8 But you shall receive power when the Holy Spirit has come upon you; and you shall be witnesses to Me in Jerusalem, and in all Judea and Samaria, and to the end of the earth.

To Enlighten

He enlightens believers.

Ephesians 1:17-23 That the God of our Lord Jesus Christ, the Father of glory,

➢ *Give Wisdom*

... may give to you the spirit of wisdom ...

➢ *Revelation*

... and revelation in the knowledge of Him, the eyes of your understanding being enlightened; that you may know ...

➢ *Know our Hope*

... what is the hope of His calling ...

➢ *Inheritance*

... what are the riches of the glory of His inheritance in the saints, and what is the exceeding greatness of His power toward us who believe ...

To Give Resurrection Power

... according to the working of His mighty power which He worked in Christ when He raised Him from the dead and seated Him at His right hand in the heavenly places, far above all principality and power and might and dominion, and every name that is named, not only in this age but also in that which is to come. And He put all things under His feet, and gave Him to be head over all things to the church, which is His body, the fullness of Him who fills all in all.

QUESTIONS FOR REVIEW

1. What are the two great promises of the first chapter of Acts?

2. What kind of things was Jesus empowered to do that the believers of today also have power to do?

3. What are four things that the Holy Spirit does for the believers?

Coming of the Holy Spirit

BAPTISM OF HOLY SPIRIT

Acts 2:1-4 Now when the Day of Pentecost had fully come, they were all with one accord in one place. And suddenly there came a sound from heaven, as of a rushing mighty wind, and it filled the whole house where they were sitting. Then there appeared to them divided tongues, as of fire, and one sat upon each of them. And they were all filled with the Holy Spirit and began to speak with other tongues, as the Spirit gave them utterance.

Evidence of Tongues

Speaking in tongues, is the evidence that a person has received the Holy Spirit. According to Luke, everyone present was filled with the Holy Spirit and began speaking in tongues. This ability was given them by the Holy Spirit.

Speaking in tongues, is an evidence of the baptism in the Holy Spirit and the scriptures say that they all received this manifestation.

Mark 16:17 And these signs will follow those who believe: In My name they will cast out demons; they will speak with new tongues ...

➤ *God's Gift*

The gift of tongues is one of God's gifts for the church. Some will be able to speak in different kinds of tongues for the edification of the body, the church.

I Corinthians 14:2,4,14 For he who speaks in a tongue does not speak to men but to God, for no one understands him; however, in the spirit he speaks mysteries. He who speaks in a tongue edifies himself, but he who prophesies edifies the church. For if I pray in a tongue, my spirit prays, but my understanding is unfruitful.

➤ *Directly to God*

Tongues is a language of prayer and praise directly from our spirit to God. When we pray in tongues we are talking to God and not to others. Others will not be able to understand these tongues.

It is a heavenly language between the human spirit and God.

➤ *Edifies Yourself*

When you pray in tongues you help yourself grow spiritually. We should pray for the ability to interpret our own prayer language.

1 Corinthians 14:13,14 Therefore let him who speaks in a tongue pray that he may interpret. For if I pray in a tongue, my spirit prays, but my understanding is unfruitful.

> *Sign to Unbelievers*

1 Corinthians 14:22 Therefore tongues are for a sign, not to those who believe but to unbelievers; but prophesying is not for unbelievers but for those who believe.

> *Gift of Spirit*

When this gift of tongues is operating in an open meeting, it will always have an interpretation so that it will edify the whole church!

1 Corinthians 14:26-28 How is it then, brethren? Whenever you come together, each of you has a psalm, has a teaching, has a tongue, has a revelation, has an interpretation. Let all things be done for edification. If anyone speaks in a tongue, let there be two or at the most three, each in turn, and let one interpret. But if there is no interpreter, let him keep silent in church, and let him speak to himself and to God.

When a "message" in tongues is given, it is no longer man speaking to God. It is God speaking to man. It is always to be used with the gift of interpretation.

> *First Gift*

Speaking in tongues is the first gift of the Holy Spirit that we are to operate in after we receive the Holy Spirit. Praying to the Father in our heavenly language will release our spirits to operate in the other eight gifts of the Spirit.

Of course, Satan has made an all-out attack on speaking in tongues. By stopping a Christian from operating in this gift of the Spirit, he can stop them from advancing to the others!

Nowhere in scripture can you find, or prove that the gift of tongues or the interpretation of tongues has ceased. The gift of tongues will cease when that which is perfect is come – when Jesus is come – and we are all speaking in one language.

> *Don't Forbid*

Speaking in tongues is the only gift that we are commanded not to forbid.

1 Corinthians 14:39 Therefore, brethren, desire earnestly to prophesy, and do not forbid to speak with tongues.

*(To study more completely the nine Gifts of the Holy Spirit use the **Supernatural Living Through the Gifts of the Holy Spirit** by A.L. and Joyce Gill)*

GOD'S PURPOSE FOR LANGUAGES

In the beginning everyone had the same language.

Unity

Genesis 11:1-6 Now the whole earth had one language and one speech. And it came to pass, as they journeyed from the east, that they found a plain in the land of Shinar, and they dwelt there. Then they said to one another, "Come, let us make bricks and bake them thoroughly." They had brick for stone, and they had asphalt for mortar. And they said, "Come, let us build ourselves a city, and a tower whose top is in the heavens; let us make a name for ourselves, lest we be scattered abroad over the face of the whole earth."

But the LORD came down to see the city and the tower which the sons of men had built. And the LORD said, "Indeed the people are one and they all have one language, and this is what they begin to do; now nothing that they propose to do will be withheld from them.

Confusion

God said that when people have one language, nothing is impossible which they can imagine. Since the fall of man, their unity was to sin. So God brought confusion on the people by changing their languages.

Genesis 11:7,8 "Come, let Us go down and there confuse their language, that they may not understand one another's speech." So the LORD scattered them abroad from there over the face of all the earth, and they ceased building the city.

Their inability to communicate with one another stopped their unity and in this situation, the building process. The unity in this case was led by Satan in the soulish realm. God caused the confusion to stop this type of unity.

Spirit-Led Unity

When believers pray in their prayer language to God, they are operating in unity, in one accord, with God. Their spirit is worshipping God.

When believers pray together in their prayer languages they will come into a unity of spirit with the other believers. In unity through the out-pouring of the Holy Spirit, believers will build a new church under God's direction.

HOLY SPIRIT RECEIVED THROUGHOUT ACTS

All through the book of Acts people were saved and then they received the gift of the Holy Spirit and they spoke in tongues.

First to Jews

Jesus had instructed the believers to wait for the infilling of the Holy Spirit before they began to step out in ministry. They were all in one accord in the upper room on the day of Pentecost when the baptism of the Holy Spirit came for the first time.

Acts 2:4 And they were all filled with the Holy Spirit and began to speak with other tongues, as the Spirit gave them utterance.

Then to Samaritans

When the deacon, Philip went to the Samaritans, they believed in Jesus and were saved. Then the apostles came from Jerusalem and laid hands on them and they were filled with the Holy Spirit.

Acts 8:15-17 Who, when they had come down, prayed for them that they might receive the Holy Spirit.

(For as yet He had fallen upon none of them. They had only been baptized in the name of the Lord Jesus.) Then they laid hands on them, and they received the Holy Spirit.

To Their Enemy

Paul, the chief persecutor of the church, was on his way to arrest more Christians in Damascus when a light flashed all around him and he fell to the ground. There he met Jesus. Then God sent Ananias to him and he laid hands on him and Paul received the baptism in the Holy Spirit.

Acts 9:17 And Ananias went his way and entered the house; and laying his hands on him he said, "Brother Saul, the Lord Jesus, who appeared to you on the road as you came, has sent me that you may receive your sight and be filled with the Holy Spirit."

To Gentiles

After Peter was given the same vision three times and instructed, "Do not call anything impure that God has made clean" God sent him to the Roman Centurion, Cornelius, his relatives and close friends.

Acts 10:44-46 While Peter was still speaking these words, the Holy Spirit fell upon all those who heard the word. And those of the circumcision who believed were astonished, as many as came with Peter, because the gift of the Holy Spirit had been poured out on the Gentiles also. For they heard them speak with tongues and magnify God.

There has been much teaching that the baptism of the Holy Spirit takes place at the moment of salvation and is not a separate work of God. It has also been taught that the gift of tongues was a manifestation that happened only at Pentecost. However, the baptism of the Holy Spirit and speaking in tongues at Caesarea, happened ten years after Pentecost.

In Ephesus

The people in the church at Ephesus received and were baptized into the Holy Spirit twenty years after Pentecost.

Acts 19:2b-6 And they said to him, "We have not so much as heard whether there is a Holy Spirit."

And he said to them, "Into what then were you baptized?"

So they said, "Into John's baptism."

Then Paul said, "John indeed baptized with a baptism of repentance, saying to the people that they should believe on Him who would come after him, that is, on Christ Jesus."

When they heard this, they were baptized in the name of the Lord Jesus. And when Paul had laid hands on them, the Holy Spirit came upon them, and they spoke with tongues and prophesied.

SYMBOLS OF HOLY GHOST

Dove

A Dove descended on Jesus when he was baptized by John in the River Jordan.

Luke 3:22 And the Holy Spirit descended in bodily form like a dove upon Him, and a voice came from heaven which said, "You are My beloved Son; in You I am well pleased."

Wind

On the day of Pentecost the Holy Spirit came with the sound of a mighty wind.

Acts 2:2 And suddenly there came a sound from heaven, as of a rushing mighty wind, and it filled the whole house where they were sitting.

Fire

On the day of Pentecost they heard the wind, and they saw fire.

Acts 2:3 Then there appeared to them divided tongues, as of fire, and one sat upon each of them.

Oil

Oil is used as a symbol of the Holy Spirit. In Hebrews He is referred to as the "oil of gladness."

Hebrews 1:9 You have loved righteousness and hated lawlessness; therefore God, Your God, has anointed You with the oil of gladness more than Your companions.

Water

The Holy Spirit is referred to as streams of "living water."

John 7:38,39 He who believes in Me, as the Scripture has said, out of his heart will flow rivers of living water. But this He spoke concerning the Spirit, whom those believing in Him would receive; for the Holy Spirit was not yet given, because Jesus was not yet glorified.

QUESTIONS FOR REVIEW

1. Define in your own words the gift of tongues.

2. Give two illustrations from Acts of the Holy Spirit coming to a body of believers.

Battle over the Name of Jesus

SATAN KNOWS SECRET

Satan has discovered the secret of the believer's effectiveness. An all out attack has been released by Satan against the power of the Holy Spirit and the authority of the name of Jesus when used by believers.

Power of Holy Spirit

Believers have been given the power of the Holy Spirit. They operate on this earth in that power but they must also have the authority of the name of Jesus.

Authority of Name of Jesus

Satan fears the power of the Holy Spirit, and he also fears the authority of the name of Jesus in the lives of the believers.

Mark 16:17,18 And these signs will follow those who believe: in My name they will cast out demons; they will speak with new tongues; they will take up serpents; and if they drink anything deadly, it will by no means hurt them; they will lay hands on the sick, and they will recover.

When Jesus told them they were to drive out demons, speak in new tongues, pick up snakes, and not be hurt by deadly poison and to place their hands on sick people, He instructed them to do so in His name. "In my name they will ..." The church was and is to operate in the power of the Holy Spirit and in the authority of the name of Jesus.

Remember, God's plan has not changed! Satan will do his best to deceive believers and keep them ignorant of their power and authority.

CRIPPLED BEGGAR HEALED

Always when an illustration is given in such detail as this, we should look for the lessons for us today.

Acts 3:1-8 Now Peter and John went up together to the temple at the hour of prayer, the ninth hour.

And a certain man lame from his mother's womb was carried, whom they laid daily at the gate of the temple which is called Beautiful, to ask alms from those who entered the temple; who, seeing Peter and John about to go into the temple, asked for alms.

And fixing his eyes on him, with John, Peter said, "Look at us." So he gave them his attention, expecting to receive something from them.

Then Peter said, "Silver and gold I do not have, but what I do have I give you: In the name of Jesus Christ of Nazareth, rise up and

walk." And he took him by the right hand and lifted him up, and immediately his feet and ankle bones received strength.

So he, leaping up, stood and walked and entered the temple with them-walking, leaping, and praising God.

Lessons for Today

➢ *On the Way*

Peter and John were on their way to the temple at the time of prayer. This miracle occurred on their way to pray. As far as we know, they were not all "prayed up." The hour of prayer means, historically, a set time of personal prayer around three o'clock in the afternoon.

Miracles are not earned by how much we pray or how "prayed up" we are. However, this is not an excuse for believers to be negligent of their prayer life.

➢ *Outside Temple*

This miracle occurred outside of the temple. It happened out on the street where the people were.

We are the body of Christ, we are the church. Wherever we are, there the church is. A miracle can happen anywhere that a believer in Jesus is. It is more important for miracles to happen outside the church since it is here that God's Word needs to be confirmed.

➢ *Jesus Waited for God's Timing*

Jesus said that He only did what He saw the Father do. He waited until it was God's time.

This man had laid beside the door to the temple daily. Jesus had often walked through this gate to the temple and so He had passed this man often, but Jesus did not heal him.

➢ *Led by Spirit*

How many times had the disciples passed this man? But this time was different, this time Peter and John looked straight at him and drew his attention to them.

We must be sensitive to the Holy Spirit's leading and His timing if we are to expect miracles to happen through our hands.

➢ *Place of Expectancy*

The man was brought into a place of expectancy. Peter made a bold statement and created that expectancy.

➢ *In Name of Jesus*

"In the name of Jesus Christ of Nazareth, rise up and walk." What Peter had to give was the name of Jesus.

➢ *Brought Man to Action*

Peter motivated the man to act. He reached down and took his hand.

The man's feet and ankles didn't become strong before the man stood. "And he took him by the right hand and lifted him up, and immediately his feet and ankle bones received strength."

➤ *Man Praised God*

The man went into the temple walking and leaping and praising God.

He praised God for all to see, and was not ashamed to give God the glory for his miracle.

➤ *All Recognized Miracle*

All recognized his healing as a miracle. They were filled with wonder and amazement.

➤ *Brought Knowledge of Jesus*

The crowd gathered and Peter taught them about a resurrected Jesus.

Acts 3:15 ... and killed the Prince of life, whom God raised from the dead, of which we are witnesses.

➤ *Faith in Name of Jesus*

First Peter made sure that the crowd knew who Jesus was and then that they knew the miracle was performed by faith in the name of Jesus.

Acts 3:16 And His name, through faith in His name, has made this man strong, whom you see and know. Yes, the faith which comes through Him has given him this perfect soundness in the presence of you all.

SATAN'S IMMEDIATE ATTACK

By what Power or Name?

You would think that the leaders in the temple would have rejoiced that a lame man was healed, but while Peter and John were still speaking they came, seized them and had them put in jail.

What was the first question they asked them?

Acts 4:7 And when they had set them in the midst, they asked, "By what power or by what name have you done this?"

Battle over Name of Jesus

Acts 4:10 ... let it be known to you all, and to all the people of Israel, that by the name of Jesus Christ of Nazareth, whom you crucified, whom God raised from the dead, by Him this man stands here before you whole.

➤ *The Dilemma*

Acts 4:16-18 Saying, "What shall we do to these men? For, indeed, that a notable miracle has been done through them is evident to all who dwell in Jerusalem, and we cannot deny it.

➤ *The Warning*

"But so that it spreads no further among the people, let us severely threaten them, that from now on they speak to no man in this name."

➤ *The Command*

And they called them and commanded them not to speak at all nor teach in the name of Jesus.

➤ *The Response*

As soon as Peter and John were released they returned to their own people and began to tell them what had happened, and then they again spoke in the name of Jesus.

Acts 4:29,30 Now, Lord, look on their threats, and grant to Your servants that with all boldness they may speak Your word, by stretching out Your hand to heal, and that signs and wonders may be done through the name of Your holy Servant Jesus.

➤ *The Punishment*

Acts 5:28 Saying, "Did we not strictly command you not to teach in this name? And look, you have filled Jerusalem with your doctrine, and intend to bring this Man's blood on us!"

The members of the Sanhedrin wished to kill the apostles for going on and speaking and working miracles in the name of Jesus. However, they followed a way of caution and had them beaten and again ordered them to stop using the name of Jesus.

Acts 5:40b ... they commanded that they should not speak in the name of Jesus, and let them go.

➤ *The Result*

Acts 5:41,42 So they departed from the presence of the council, rejoicing that they were counted worthy to suffer shame for His name. And daily in the temple, and in every house, they did not cease teaching and preaching Jesus as the Christ.

SAUL (PAUL) AND NAME OF JESUS

Persecuted Others

The first persecution of the believers was for calling on the name of Jesus. According to Ananias, the way that Saul knew whom to arrest was by their use of the name of Jesus.

Acts 9:13,14 Then Ananias answered, "Lord, I have heard from many about this man, how much harm he has done to Your saints in Jerusalem. And here he has authority from the chief priests to bind all who call on Your name."

Chosen to Carry Name

God sent Ananias to Saul because God had chosen Saul to carry the name of Jesus before the Gentiles, before the Gentile kings and also before the people of Israel. Saul would also suffer for using the name of Jesus just as he had caused suffering to others.

Acts 9:15,16 But the Lord said to him, "Go, for he is a chosen vessel of Mine to bear My name before Gentiles, kings, and the children of Israel. For I will show him how many things he must suffer for My name's sake."

Willing to Die for Name

Paul was willing to die for the name of Jesus.

Acts 21:13 Then Paul answered, "What do you mean by weeping and breaking my heart? For I am ready not only to be bound, but also to die at Jerusalem for the name of the Lord Jesus."

Writes About Name

Paul knew the power of the name of Jesus. He knew it as one who had fought that power and lost. He knew it as one who had been saved through the name of Jesus. Over and over, Paul wrote about the name of Jesus.

Romans 10:13 For "whoever calls upon the name of the Lord shall be saved."

1 Corinthians 5:4 In the name of our Lord Jesus Christ, when you are gathered together, along with my spirit, with the power of our Lord Jesus Christ ...

Philippians 2:9,10 Therefore God also has highly exalted Him and given Him the name which is above every name, that at the name of Jesus every knee should bow, of those in heaven, and of those on earth, and of those under the earth ...

Colossians 3:17 And whatever you do in word or deed, do all in the name of the Lord Jesus, giving thanks to God the Father through Him.

THE NAME OF JESUS

Why did the early believers die rather then give up using the name of Jesus?

Why did the religious leaders attack the name of Jesus from the very first instances of its use?

Both the believers and the religious leaders understood the power that came from using that name.

Brings Salvation

It is through the name of Jesus that we are brought to salvation.

Acts 2:21 And it shall come to pass that whoever calls on the name of the Lord shall be saved.

Acts 2:38 Then Peter said to them, "Repent, and let every one of you be baptized in the name of Jesus Christ for the remission of sins; and you shall receive the gift of the Holy Spirit."

Victory

> It is through the name of Jesus that we are able to fulfill the Great Commission and bring salvation to the whole world.
>
> It is through the name of Jesus that demons are driven out and people are set free.

Healing

> The name of Jesus brings healing.
>
> **Acts 3:16 And His name, through faith in His name, has made this man strong, whom you see and know. Yes, the faith which comes through Him has given him this perfect soundness in the presence of you all.**

Relationship with God

> We can approach God the Father because of what Jesus has done for us and by using His name.
>
> **John 16:23 And in that day you will ask Me nothing. Most assuredly, I say to you, whatever you ask the Father in My name He will give you.**
>
> **Ephesians 5:20 Giving thanks always for all things to God the Father in the name of our Lord Jesus Christ ...**

RESERVED FOR BELIEVERS ONLY

> The use of the name of Jesus is reserved for the church. The name of Jesus becomes powerful when used in faith.

Seven Sons of Sceva

> There were seven sons who tried using the name of Jesus without knowing Jesus and they certainly ran into trouble.
>
> **Acts 19:13-16 Then some of the itinerant Jewish exorcists took it upon themselves to call the name of the Lord Jesus over those who had evil spirits, saying, "We adjure you by the Jesus whom Paul preaches."**
>
> **Also there were seven sons of Sceva, a Jewish chief priest, who did so. And the evil spirit answered and said, "Jesus I know, and Paul I know; but who are you?"**
>
> **Then the man in whom the evil spirit was leaped on them, overpowered them, and prevailed against them, so that they fled out of that house naked and wounded.**

Naked, Bleeding, Defeated

> The name of Jesus cannot be used like a talisman or a charm. The power of using the name of Jesus is almost beyond description when used in faith by a true believer, but is of no power when used by an unbeliever.

Name Held in High Honor

> Those who tried to use the name of Jesus without the right to do so were discredited, but the name of Jesus was held

in even higher honor and many came to know Jesus through this incident.

Acts 19:17,18 This became known both to all Jews and Greeks dwelling in Ephesus; and fear fell on them all, and the name of the Lord Jesus was magnified. And many who had believed came confessing and telling their deeds.

Perversion of His Name

Satan knows the power of the name of Jesus when spoken in faith by believers. Therefore, one of his attacks has been to pervert, weaken, blaspheme and destroy the power of that name.

His name is often used as a swear word. His name is uttered often in blasphemy.

Do you ever hear an unsaved person utter the name of the founders of other religions as a swear word? Why not?

Those names, or any other name of a false god have no power. Satan has no reason to bring discredit to those names. Instead, he will hold them up in honor. They belong to him.

CALLED BY HIS NAME

As Christians, we are given wonderful blessings – blessings beyond description. There are also tremendous responsibilities placed on those who are called by the name of Christ – those who are called Christians.

To Bring Glory to God

Paul when writing to Timothy spoke of this.

2 Thessalonians 1:12 That the name of our Lord Jesus Christ may be glorified in you, and you in Him, according to the grace of our God and the Lord Jesus Christ.

Our lives are to bring glory to God.

Not to Bring Reproach

In writing to the Jews Paul upbraided them for the reproach they brought to the name of God. The same warning applies to those who carry the name of "Christian."

Romans 2:17-24 Indeed you are called a Jew, and rest on the law, and make your boast in God, and know His will, and approve the things that are excellent, being instructed out of the law, and are confident that you yourself are a guide to the blind, a light to those who are in darkness, an instructor of the foolish, a teacher of babes, having the form of knowledge and truth in the law.

You, therefore, who teach another, do you not teach yourself? You who preach that a man should not steal, do you steal? You who say, "Do not commit adultery," do you commit adultery? You who abhor idols, do you rob temples?

You who make your boast in the law, do you dishonor God through breaking the law? For "The name of God is blasphemed among the Gentiles because of you," as it is written.

To Turn from Wickedness

Paul wrote to Timothy.

2 Timothy 2:19 Nevertheless the solid foundation of God stands, having this seal: "The Lord knows those who are His," and, "Let everyone who names the name of Christ depart from iniquity."

BELIEVE IN JESUS AND BELIEVE IN HIS NAME

Just as we believe in Jesus for our salvation, we are to believe in the power and authority of His name to walk in victory in our daily lives.

It is interesting the number of times in the New Testament we are told to call on the name of Jesus and to believe in the name of Jesus. Why are we not just told to call on Jesus or just to believe in Jesus? Why are we continuously instructed to call on, or believe in His name?

Jesus purchased our salvation through His death on the cross. Through His life as a perfect man, through His death and through His resurrection, He won back from Satan the authority to rule this earth. By using His name believers have the authority to rule this earth now!

Jesus has given us His name. We are to speak and act in His name. When we do this and have faith in the power of His name, we can do anything that Jesus did. We can even do greater things than He did!

When Jesus said He would build His church He did not leave us powerless to struggle through our time on this earth. How can we be victorious over the devil and his demons if we have no power and authority? Jesus has given us the Holy Spirit so that we would have power and He has given us the right to use His name so that we would have authority.

QUESTIONS FOR REVIEW

1. How is the name of Jesus important to you?

2. Give some of the blessings of having the name of Jesus. Give some of the responsibilities.

3. What happened to the sons of Sceva? Why?

Lesson Five

Jesus' Plan for the Church

JESUS WILL BUILD HIS CHURCH

It is Jesus, not man, who is to build the church.

Matthew 16:18 And I also say to you that you are Peter, and on this rock I will build My church, and the gates of Hades shall not prevail against it.

For many years man has been trying to build the church using his own traditional patterns and methods. If Jesus is to build His church, it is necessary that we lay aside our own ideas and traditions and let Jesus reveal His plan to us through His Word.

Includes Every Believer

➢ *To Witness*

Every believer is to be a witness for Jesus Christ.

Acts 1:8 But you shall receive power when the Holy Spirit has come upon you; and you shall be witnesses to Me in Jerusalem, and in all Judea and Samaria, and to the end of the earth.

➢ *Do Things Jesus Did*

Every believer is to do the things that Jesus did.

John 14:12 Most assuredly, I say to you, he who believes in Me, the works that I do he will do also; and greater works than these he will do, because I go to My Father.

➢ *To Preach*

Every believer is to preach (proclaim or share) the gospel.

Mark 16:15 And He said to them, "Go into all the world and preach the gospel to every creature ..."

➢ *Expect Miraculous*

Every believer is to expect miraculous signs to follow him.

Mark 16:17,18 And these signs will follow those who believe: in My name they will cast out demons; they will speak with new tongues; they will take up serpents; and if they drink anything deadly, it will by no means hurt them; they will lay hands on the sick, and they will recover.

➢ *Equipped for Ministry*

All of God's people are to be prepared for the work of the ministry.

Ephesians 4:12 For the equipping of the saints for the work of ministry, for the edifying of the body of Christ ...

FIVEFOLD MINISTRY – FUNCTIONS, NOT TITLES

When Jesus ascended to His Father, he gave gifts to men.

Ephesians 4:8-13 Therefore He says: "When He ascended on high, He led captivity captive, and gave gifts to men." (Now this, "He ascended"–what does it mean but that He also first descended into the lower parts of the earth? He who descended is also the One who ascended far above all the heavens, that He might fill all things.)

And He Himself gave some to be apostles, some prophets, some evangelists, and some pastors and teachers, for the equipping of the saints for the work of ministry, for the edifying of the body of Christ, till we all come to the unity of the faith and the knowledge of the Son of God, to a perfect man, to the measure of the stature of the fullness of Christ ...

Apostle, prophet, evangelist, pastor or teacher are not to be titles of rank or position in the church. Instead they are functions. Each ministry function has its own important part in edifying the body of Christ.

When Paul wrote the Epistles, he often began by saying, "Paul, an apostle" denoting a ministry gifting or function in the body of Christ. He did not say "The Apostle Paul" which would have indicated a title.

Appointed by God

1 Corinthians 12:27,28 Now you are the body of Christ, and members individually. And God has appointed these in the church: first apostles, second prophets, third teachers, after that miracles, then gifts of healings, helps, administrations, varieties of tongues.

All of the five ministry giftings must be active and functioning in each local church if the believers are to be prepared for works of service and built up to maturity in the full measure of Christ.

Servants

If we are to be called of God into the fivefold ministry, we must first of all be servants to the body of Christ.

Jesus functioned in all five of the ministry giftings as our example. That example was one of a servant.

John 13:3-5 Jesus, knowing that the Father had given all things into His hands, and that He had come from God and was going to God, rose from supper and laid aside His garments, took a towel and girded Himself. After that, He poured water into a basin and began to wash the disciples' feet, and to wipe them with the towel with which He was girded.

vs.12-17 So when He had washed their feet, taken His garments, and sat down again, He said to them, "Do you know what I have done to you? You call me Teacher and Lord, and you say well, for so I am. If I then, your Lord and Teacher, have washed your feet, you also ought to wash one another's feet. For I have given you an example, that you should do as I have done to you. Most

assuredly, I say to you, a servant is not greater than his master; nor is he who is sent greater than he who sent him. If you know these things, happy are you if you do them."

APOSTLE

Defined

The Greek word "apostolos," translated "apostle," means "one sent forth, a sent one."

An apostle is one who is sent out with the authority to establish churches and to strengthen existing churches in the foundational doctrines and practical teachings from the Word of God. He will minister with boldness and authority and with revelation-knowledge by the Holy Spirit.

Functions

He will function in all of the ministry giftings and operate in all of the gifts of the Holy Spirit.

An apostle will minister from a deep personal relationship with God and will have a "father" relationship to those to whom he ministers. Signs, wonders and healing miracles will be continually manifested.

His ministry gifting will be recognized and received as a relationship of the Spirit to certain churches and other ministries. It will not be a relationship of human organization or denomination. From this spiritual relationship, the apostle will govern and bring any necessary discipline, accountability, stability and protection from deception into the lives of believers, ministries and churches.

The apostle will function closely with the ministry of the prophet in appointing and ordaining elders and confirming those chosen to be deacons. Together with the prophet, he will confirm God's call on certain believer's lives and establish them into functioning in that ministry gifting. He will impart and release believers into operating in the gifts of the Holy Spirit by the laying on of hands.

The apostle will minister and speak with authority but he will be a man under authority because he is accountable to the other apostles and elders from the local church where he was sent out.

Examples

Paul and Barnabas are good examples of apostles:

Acts 13:2,3 As they ministered to the Lord and fasted, the Holy Spirit said, "Now separate to Me Barnabas and Saul for the work to which I have called them." Then, having fasted and prayed, and laid hands on them, they sent them away.

Romans 15:20 And so I have made it my aim to preach the gospel, not where Christ was named, lest I should build on another man's foundation ...

Acts 14:23 So when they had appointed elders in every church, and prayed with fasting, they commended them to the Lord in whom they had believed.

PROPHET

Defined

The Greek word "propheteuo," translated "prophet," means "to foretell events, and to speak under inspiration."

A prophet is one who speaks for God. He has been given the distinctive ministry of representing God before men. This revelation, while in total harmony with Scripture, will give direction, confirm guidance and vision and give insight into the Word of God. The Prophet will reveal facts about people's lives, rebuke, judge, correct, warn and reveal future events.

Functions

A prophet will minister under a greater level of the prophetic anointing and with greater detail and accuracy than will one who is simply operating in the spiritual gift of prophecy. The word from a prophet will often contain revelation that goes beyond edification, exhortation and comfort than can come as any believer prophesies.

A prophet will often minister together with an apostle in laying spiritual foundations and establishing and strengthening churches.

Ephesians 2:20 Having been built on the foundation of the apostles and prophets, Jesus Christ Himself being the chief cornerstone ...

Example

Agabus is a good example of a prophet.

Acts 21:10,11 And as we stayed many days, a certain prophet named Agabus came down from Judea. When he had come to us, he took Paul's belt, bound his own hands and feet, and said, "Thus says the Holy Spirit, 'So shall the Jews at Jerusalem bind the man who owns this belt, and deliver him into the hands of the Gentiles.'"

EVANGELIST

Defined

The Greek word "euangelistes," translated "evangelist," means "a messenger of good tidings."

Function

The evangelist is on the front lines of God's army today. He has a burning desire to tell everyone he sees about

Jesus. He has a heart that is continually reaching out to the lost of this world. Everywhere he goes, he is witnessing or preaching to people about Jesus with signs following.

He is actively involved in training other believers for miracle evangelism and then mobilizing them into evangelistic outreach ministries. He will keep the vision of local, national and world evangelism stirred up in the hearts of the believers in every church.

While evangelism is the ministry and responsibility of every believer, the evangelist ministers in a higher level of anointing in this area. He is a specialist in evangelism. His primary responsibility is to prepare all believers to do the work of evangelism.

Example

Philip is a great example of an evangelist.

Acts 8:5-8 Then Philip went down to the city of Samaria and preached Christ to them. And the multitudes with one accord heeded the things spoken by Philip, hearing and seeing the miracles which he did. For unclean spirits, crying with a loud voice, came out of many who were possessed; and many who were paralyzed and lame were healed. And there was great joy in that city.

Acts 8:12 But when they believed Philip as he preached the things concerning the kingdom of God and the name of Jesus Christ, both men and women were baptized.

PASTOR (SHEPHERD)

Definition

The Greek word "poimen," translated "pastor," means "shepherd, one who tends herds or flocks, guides as well as feeds the flock, overseer." Poimen is used eighteen times in the New Testament. Only in Ephesians four is it translated "pastor." The other seventeen times it is more accurately translated "shepherd."

Function

➤ *Lead*

A shepherd will lead the sheep.

John 10:4 And when he brings out his own sheep, he goes before them; and the sheep follow him, for they know his voice.

➤ *Closely Relate*

A shepherd will have a close personal relationship with his sheep.

Isaiah 40:11 He will feed His flock like a shepherd; He will gather the lambs with His arm, and carry them in His bosom, and gently lead those who are with young.

John 10:11 I am the good shepherd. The good shepherd gives His life for the sheep.

> *Feed Sheep*

A shepherd will feed the sheep.

John 21:15-17 So when they had eaten breakfast, Jesus said to Simon Peter, "Simon, son of Jonah, do you love Me more than these?"

He said to Him, "Yes, Lord; You know that I love You."

He said to him, "Feed My lambs."

He said to him again a second time, "Simon, son of Jonah, do you love Me?"

He said to Him, "Yes, Lord; You know that I love You."

He said to him, "Tend My sheep." He said to him the third time, "Simon, son of Jonah, do you love Me?"

Peter was grieved because He said to him the third time, "Do you love Me?" And he said to Him, "Lord, You know all things; You know that I love You."

Jesus said to him, "Feed My sheep.

TEACHER

Definition

The Greek word "didaskalo," means "an instructor."

A teacher is one who instructs, and by his teaching causes others to learn. His teaching involves exposition and explanation of scripture and instruction in doctrine to others. By so doing, he will be making disciples.

Matthew 28:19,20 Go therefore and make disciples of all the nations, baptizing them in the name of the Father and of the Son and of the Holy Spirit, teaching them to observe all things that I have commanded you; and lo, I am with you always, even to the end of the age. Amen.

Functions

A teacher will teach new believers.

> *Teach new Believers*

Acts 11:21-26 And the hand of the Lord was with them, and a great number believed and turned to the Lord. Then news of these things came to the ears of the church in Jerusalem, and they sent out Barnabas to go as far as Antioch. When he came and had seen the grace of God, he was glad, and encouraged them all that with purpose of heart they should continue with the Lord. For he was a good man, full of the Holy Spirit and of faith. And a great many people were added to the Lord.

Then Barnabas departed for Tarsus to seek Saul. And when he had found him, he brought him to Antioch. So it was that for a whole year they assembled with the church and taught a great

many people. And the disciples were first called Christians in Antioch.

➤ *Teach Faith*

A teacher will teach believers to live by faith.

1 Timothy 2:7 For which I was appointed a preacher and an apostle–I am speaking the truth in Christ and not lying–a teacher of the Gentiles in faith and truth.

➤ *Teach by Holy Spirit*

A teacher will teach by the anointing of the Holy Spirit.

1 John 2:20 But you have an anointing from the Holy One, and you know all things.

1 John 2:27 But the anointing which you have received from Him abides in you, and you do not need that anyone teach you; but as the same anointing teaches you concerning all things, and is true, and is not a lie, and just as it has taught you, you will abide in Him.

1 Corinthians 2:13 These things we also speak, not in words which man's wisdom teaches but which the Holy Spirit teaches, comparing spiritual things with spiritual.

➤ *With Authority*

A teacher teaches with authority.

Matthew 7:28,29 And so it was, when Jesus had ended these sayings, that the people were astonished at His teaching, for He taught them as one having authority, and not as the scribes.

➤ *Multiplies Himself*

A teacher directs his ministry to reliable men who will multiply themselves in the lives of others.

2 Timothy 2:2 And the things that you have heard from me among many witnesses, commit these to faithful men who will be able to teach others also.

ELDERS AND DEACONS

Elders (also called overseers) and deacons are the only two offices that were established by God to reside in the local church.

Philippians 1:1 Paul and Timothy, servants of Jesus Christ, To all the saints in Christ Jesus who are in Philippi, with the bishops and deacons ...

Elders (Overseers)

The office of an elder, or overseer, is for ruling or governing the local church. They are to be chosen by God and appointed by the apostles.

1 Timothy 3:1 This is a faithful saying: If a man desires the position of a bishop, he desires a good work.

Acts 14:23 **So when they had appointed elders in every church, and prayed with fasting, they commended them to the Lord in whom they had believed.**

Deacons

The office of a deacon is for serving. They were chosen by the believers and confirmed by the apostles.

Acts 6:2-4,6 **Then the twelve summoned the multitude of the disciples and said, "It is not desirable that we should leave the word of God and serve tables. Therefore, brethren, seek out from among you seven men of good reputation, full of the Holy Spirit and wisdom, whom we may appoint over this business; but we will give ourselves continually to prayer and to the ministry of the word."**

Whom they set before the apostles; and when they had prayed, they laid hands on them.

1 Timothy 3:10 **But let these also first be proved; then let them serve as deacons, being found blameless.**

UNDERSTANDING OFFICE – FUNCTION OF ELDERS (OVERSEERS)

Definition

The Greek word "presbuteros" means elder, older person or a senior. In the Old Testament it referred to the members of the Sanhedrin or the leaders of the synagogues. This word was most often used in the New Testament Church when writing to Hebrew believers since they understood the Old Testament pattern for "elders."

Acts 14:23 **So when they had appointed elders in every church, and prayed with fasting, they commended them to the Lord in whom they had believed.**

The Greek word "episkopos" means an overseer, a superintendent or a guardian. It is used five times in the New Testament and is consistently translated "overseer" in the New International Version. It was translated "bishop" four of these times in the King James Version. The word "overseer" is the actual translation. This word was most often used when writing to Greek believers because that was the word for spiritual leadership to which they would most readily relate.

Acts 20:28a **Therefore take heed to yourselves and to all the flock, among which the Holy Spirit has made you overseers ...**

Functions

There is no scriptural distinction in function between these two words. They refer to the same office in the local church. There was no ecclesiastical hierarchy in or over the local church. Each church was separate and autonomous.

Church government, instead of being an organization, association or denomination of men, was a relationship in the Spirit between men who are called to be apostles and the elders of a local church. The local church functioned as a sending body, but was never considered a "mother church" that would dominate, rule or restrict another church.

As the apostles and prophets laid foundations, established churches and appointed elders in every church, they established deep spiritual relationships. These relationships were the only connection outside of the local churches and they were to people who functioned in the fivefold ministry, not to other churches or denominations.

A foundation was first laid by the ministry of an apostle and a prophet in establishing a new local church. The apostles would then appoint elders in that church. The elders were the ruling body that directed the affairs of the local church.

1 Timothy 5:17 Let the elders who rule well be counted worthy of double honor, especially those who labor in the word and doctrine.

Fivefold Elders

All fivefold ministers were elders. We see examples of this in Peter and John.

1 Peter 5:1 The elders who are among you I exhort, I who am a fellow elder and a witness of the sufferings of Christ, and also a partaker of the glory that will be revealed ...

3 John 1:1 THE ELDER, To the beloved Gaius, whom I love in truth ...

Those who Jesus has given to His church as apostles, prophets, evangelists, pastors and teachers are to function together to "prepare God's people for works of service." These ministry functions are never referred to in the scriptures as an "office." However, each one of them stood in the office of an "elder" in the church.

Ministry of Elders

Elders are to function in each local assembly to shepherd and feed the flock to whom they were given oversight.

1 Peter 5:1-3 The elders who are among you I exhort, I who am a fellow elder and a witness of the sufferings of Christ, and also a partaker of the glory that will be revealed: shepherd the flock of God which is among you, serving as overseers, not by constraint but willingly, not for dishonest gain but eagerly; nor as being lords over those entrusted to you, but being examples to the flock ...

ELDERS ARE FIVEFOLD MINISTRIES

Those whom God placed in the five ministry giftings listed in Ephesians four, were given a certain grace and anointing to equip the saints. It seems to be evident that those chosen to shepherd, feed and oversee the flock would need the grace and anointing of the fivefold ministry.

It appears that the elders of the local church were those whom God had called into the fivefold ministry. Each of them met all of the biblical qualifications for eldership. These elders were charged with the responsibility of directing "the affairs of the church."

1 Timothy 5:17 Let the elders who rule well be counted worthy of double honor, especially those who labor in the word and doctrine.

While one of the qualifications of the elders is that they are "able to teach," we are not told that all functioned in a preaching or teaching ministry within the local church.

Functions

After the foundations had been laid by the apostle and prophet and they had been appointed elders in the local church, those whom God chose to function as pastors and teachers were appointed, recognized and released into their ministry by the laying on of hands by the apostle and prophets and other elders.

As the believers were built up in the Word and discipled by the ministry of those who functioned as pastors and teachers, those whom God had chosen to function as evangelists were also appointed, recognized and released into ministry by the laying on the hands of the elders. The evangelist trained and mobilized the believers in the local church into reaching out in miracle evangelism.

The body could only mature and be equipped for the works of service by being ministered to by each of the fivefold ministry giftings.

Leading Elder

It is obvious therefore that the elders appointed in each local assembly were those whom God had called to function in one of the fivefold ministry giftings, and the eldership of a local assembly was never limited to one individual. However, God has always raised up Spiritual leadership as He did Moses to lead His people. This leadership was referred to as the "angel" (messenger) of the local church in the book of Revelation.

➢ *"Angel" or Messenger*

Revelation 2:1 To the angel of the church of Ephesus write, 'These things says He who holds the seven stars in His right hand, who walks in the midst of the seven golden lampstands ...'

➢ *James, a Leading Elder*

James appears to have been the leading elder, who headed the other elders at the Jerusalem Church. All of the elders met with the apostles to consider a question of doctrine.

Acts 15:6 So the apostles and elders came together to consider this matter.

Acts 15:13 And after they had become silent, James answered, saying, "Men and brethren, listen to me ...

All of the elders were involved in considering the doctrinal question that had become an issue. However, it was James as the head or leading elder that had to make the final judgment.

Headship in Church

Jesus is the head of the Church. However under the headship of Jesus, there was also a God ordained headship over the local church. This headship was found in the leading elder who, together with all of the elders, functioned to "direct the affairs of the church," and "to prepare God's people for works of service."

➢ *New Testament Pattern*

If our traditional pattern of church government does not comply with the New Testament pattern, we must be willing to take steps to change our pattern. God is restoring the fivefold ministry to His church in our time.

➢ *Change Without Conflict*

When we receive this revelation, we must allow time for this revelation to be received by the local assembly before attempting to make the necessary changes. By doing this we can avoid the possibility of strife and conflict. Decisions regarding church government are to be a function of the one recognized as the apostle (foundation layer) together with the leading elder and elders of the church. It is not to become an issue that could lead to division among the assembly of the believers.

FLATTERING TITLES

The fivefold ministry giftings are functions and not titles. We are not to address one another by flattering titles.

Matthew 23:6-12 They love the best places at feasts, the best seats in the synagogues, greetings in the marketplaces, and to be called by men, 'Rabbi, Rabbi.' But you, do not be called 'Rabbi'; for One is your Teacher, the Christ, and you are all brethren. Do not call anyone on earth your father; for One is your Father, He who is in heaven.

And do not be called teachers; for One is your Teacher, the Christ.

But he who is greatest among you shall be your servant. And whoever exalts himself will be abased, and he who humbles himself will be exalted.

All Brothers

Jesus said "you are all brothers." Paul began his letters, "Paul, an apostle," never "The Apostle Paul" because the word "apostle" referred to his function in the body of Christ.

Peter referred to Paul as a brother.

2 Peter 3:15 And account that the longsuffering of our Lord is salvation-as also our beloved brother Paul, according to the wisdom given to him, has written to you ...

Instead of "Reverend, Doctor, Teacher, Father, Pastor" how much better it is to call one another "brother." Even Jesus went by His first name. We are all servants to one another.

Respect Office

While, we are clearly not to address one another by flattering titles, we must still respect those who God has called into the office of an elder. We must honor and receive with respect those whom God has given to function in each of the fivefold ministry giftings in His church.

Matthew 10:40 He who receives you receives Me, and he who receives Me receives Him who sent Me.

While Jesus said, "you are all brothers," we must at the same time recognize and receive with respect each of those who are called to function in the fivefold ministry. If we therefore choose to refer to our pastor as "Brother James," we should at the same time recognize and respect Him as "our pastor." Obviously, the same should apply to each of the other ministry giftings.

*(For more in-depth teaching on the subject of the fivefold ministry and church government, we suggest you study **The Ministries Gifts** by A.L. Gill.)*

QUESTIONS FOR REVIEW

1. What is the primary function of the fivefold ministry given in Ephesians 4:8-13?

2. List the five ministry giftings and briefly describe each of their functions.

3. Describe the function of elders and deacons in the local church.

Lesson Six

An Example for Today

JESUS BUILDS NEW TESTAMENT CHURCH

When Jesus first mentioned the church, He made two statements about it that are very important. Jesus said that He would build the church. Today, we must realize that we are only the instruments through which Jesus is building His church.

Over the years Christians have heard Jesus' Great Commission and have tried to go and do it in their own strength, ability and wisdom. For years, men have been trying to build the church by their own methods and traditions. But Jesus said He, not the believers, would build His church.

Matthew 16:18 And I also say to you that you are Peter, and on this rock I will build My church, and the gates of Hades shall not prevail against it.

The second thing that Jesus said about His church was that the gates of Hades, (all the governments of Satan), would not prevail against it.

Jesus is going to build the church and it will be a powerful church. That is the type of church we see all through the book of Acts.

Baptism with Holy Spirit

Jesus sent the Holy Spirit to give us the leading, the teaching, the abilities we would need to be part of the "building team" for His church.

Luke 3:16 John answered, saying to them all, "I indeed baptize you with water; but One mightier than I is coming, whose sandal strap I am not worthy to loose. He will baptize you with the Holy Spirit and with fire."

Acts 1:8 But you shall receive power when the Holy Spirit has come upon you; and you shall be witnesses to Me in Jerusalem, and in all Judea and Samaria, and to the end of the earth.

John 14:16,17 And I will pray the Father, and He will give you another Helper, that He may abide with you forever, even the Spirit of truth, whom the world cannot receive, because it neither sees Him nor knows Him; but you know Him, for He dwells with you and will be in you.

Teaching of Word

When anyone is teaching or preaching, it is well to remember that it is the Holy Spirit that is the real teacher. We can present the facts but it is the Holy Spirit that takes them into the listener and makes them a part of his, or her, life.

John 14:26 But the Helper, the Holy Spirit, whom the Father will send in My name, He will teach you all things, and bring to your remembrance all things that I said to you.

When Paul spent two years teaching in a Bible school, the results were that all the Jews and Greeks in Asia heard the Good News.

Acts 19:9,10 But when some were hardened and did not believe, but spoke evil of the Way before the multitude, he departed from them and withdrew the disciples, reasoning daily in the school of Tyrannus. And this continued for two years, so that all who dwelt in Asia heard the word of the Lord Jesus, both Jews and Greeks.

Teaching will allow the word of God to spread and grow in power.

Acts 19:20 So the word of the Lord grew mightily and prevailed.

Perseverance

Paul is one of the greatest examples of a believer going on no matter what Satan threw at him. He gives the list of things that happened to him for the gospel's sake.

2 Corinthians 11:23-27 Are they ministers of Christ?–I speak as a fool–I am more:
in labors more abundant,
in stripes above measure,
in prisons more frequently,
in deaths often.

From the Jews five times I received forty stripes minus one.
Three times I was beaten with rods;
once I was stoned;
three times I was shipwrecked;
a night and a day I have been in the deep;
in journeys often, in perils of waters,
in perils of robbers,
in perils of my own countrymen,
in perils of the Gentiles,
in perils in the city,
in perils in the wilderness,
in perils in the sea,
in perils among false brethren;
in weariness and toil,
in sleeplessness often,
in hunger and thirst,
in fastings often,
in cold and nakedness ...

Paul had made up his mind that he would do absolutely anything to take the name of Jesus to others, even if it cost him his life.

Acts 21:10-13 And as we stayed many days, a certain prophet named Agabus came down from Judea. When he had come to us, he took Paul's belt, bound his own hands and feet, and said, "Thus says the Holy Spirit, 'So shall the Jews at Jerusalem bind the man who owns this belt, and deliver him into the hands of the Gentiles.' "

And when we heard these things, both we and those from that place pleaded with him not to go up to Jerusalem. Then Paul answered, "What do you mean by weeping and breaking my heart? For I am ready not only to be bound, but also to die at Jerusalem for the name of the Lord Jesus."

Signs, Wonders, Miracles

In previous lessons we have studied how God used signs, wonder and miracles to further the gospel throughout the whole world.

Acts 19:11,12 Now God worked unusual miracles by the hands of Paul, so that even handkerchiefs or aprons were brought from his body to the sick, and the diseases left them and the evil spirits went out of them.

True Repentance

Acts 19:18 And many who had believed came confessing and telling their deeds.

Multiplication

We are to tell people about Jesus everywhere we go. We are to tell them Who He is and what He has done. We are the images of God. We are the mirror through which the Lord can be seen by the unbelieving world.

Psalms 105:1,2 Oh, give thanks to the LORD! Call upon His name; Make known His deeds among the peoples.

Sing to Him, sing psalms to Him; Talk of all His wondrous works.

Isaiah 8:18 Here am I and the children whom the LORD has given me! We are for signs and wonders in Israel From the LORD of hosts, Who dwells in Mount Zion.

Since the fall of Adam and Eve, all mankind has been searching for God. It is in man's spirit to seek the supernatural. As believers, we have the revelation of God and the manifestation of the power of God for which the world is seeking.

Mark 5:19 However, Jesus did not permit him, but said to him, "Go home to your friends, and tell them what great things the Lord has done for you, and how He has had compassion on you."

Every believer is to be an instant witness. We can tell about the experiences of our own life – how we found God – the peace in our life – the miracles we have seen – and how much God loves each one of us.

The world can be won by miracle evangelism as every believer continues to witness and proclaim the Gospel with miraculous signs following.

Acts 19:17 This became known both to all Jews and Greeks dwelling in Ephesus; and fear fell on them all, and the name of the Lord Jesus was magnified.

SEVEN BAPTISMS

The word "baptism" means to be totally identified with.

There are seven baptisms mentioned in the scripture – the baptism:

- ➢ of Moses
- ➢ of John
- ➢ of Jesus, (unique just to Him)
- ➢ of fire
- ➢ of Holy Spirit (into the body of Jesus)
- ➢ in the Holy Spirit by Jesus (the power to witness)
- ➢ of water (A testimony of our identification with Christ)

Of Moses

The children of Israel became totally identified with Moses in the crossing of the Red Sea and as God led them through the wilderness under a cloud by day and a pillar of fire by night.

1 Corinthians 10:1-4 Moreover, brethren, I do not want you to be unaware that all our fathers were under the cloud, all passed through the sea, all were baptized into Moses in the cloud and in the sea, all ate the same spiritual food, and all drank the same spiritual drink. For they drank of that spiritual Rock that followed them, and that Rock was Christ.

Of John

The baptism of John was unto repentance.

Matthew 3:11 I indeed baptize you with water unto repentance, but He who is coming after me is mightier than I, whose sandals I am not worthy to carry. He will baptize you with the Holy Spirit and fire.

Of Jesus

The baptism of Jesus was a unique baptism for Him alone. He was not baptized unto repentance even though He was baptized by John. That is why John argued with Him.

Matthew 3:13-16 Then Jesus came from Galilee to John at the Jordan to be baptized by him. And John tried to prevent Him, saying, "I have need to be baptized by You, and are You coming to me?"

But Jesus answered and said to him, "Permit it to be so now, for thus it is fitting for us to fulfill all righteousness." Then he allowed Him.

The Holy Spirit came on Jesus as He was baptized and miracles were manifested in His life from that time forward.

By Fire

John prophesied that Jesus would baptize with the Holy Spirit and fire.

Matthew 3:11b,12 ... but He who is coming after me is mightier than I, whose sandals I am not worthy to carry. He will baptize you with the Holy Spirit and fire.

His winnowing fan is in His hand, and He will thoroughly purge His threshing floor, and gather His wheat into the barn; but He will burn up the chaff with unquenchable fire.

In the baptism with fire, the works of the flesh, "chaff," are burned up and removed from our lives. Only the real fruit of the Spirit, "wheat," will be left.

By Holy Spirit

We are baptized into Christ by the Holy Spirit.

Romans 6:3 Or do you not know that as many of us as were baptized into Christ Jesus were baptized into His death?

1 Corinthians 12:13 For by one Spirit we were all baptized into one body-whether Jews or Greeks, whether slaves or free-and have all been made to drink into one Spirit.

Titus 3:5 Not by works of righteousness which we have done, but according to His mercy He saved us, through the washing of regeneration and renewing of the Holy Spirit ...

By Jesus

We are baptized by Jesus into the Holy Spirit.

Luke 3:16 John answered, saying to them all, "I indeed baptize you with water; but One mightier than I is coming, whose sandal strap I am not worthy to loose. He will baptize you with the Holy Spirit and with fire."

Acts 1:4,5,8 And being assembled together with them, He commanded them not to depart from Jerusalem, but to wait for the Promise of the Father, "which," He said, "you have heard from Me; for John truly baptized with water, but you shall be baptized with the Holy Spirit not many days from now.

But you shall receive power when the Holy Spirit has come upon you; and you shall be witnesses to Me in Jerusalem, and in all Judea and Samaria, and to the end of the earth."

By Water

Water baptism is identification with Christ in His death, burial and resurrection.

Romans 6:3,4 Or do you not know that as many of us as were baptized into Christ Jesus were baptized into His death? Therefore we were buried with Him through baptism into death, that just as Christ was raised from the dead by the glory of the Father, even so we also should walk in newness of life.

BAPTISM COMMANDED

We are commanded to repent and be baptized.

Acts 2:38-41 Then Peter said to them, "Repent, and let every one of you be baptized in the name of Jesus Christ for the remission of sins; and you shall receive the gift of the Holy Spirit. For the promise is to you and to your children, and to all who are afar off, as many as the Lord our God will call."

And with many other words he testified and exhorted them, saying, "Be saved from this perverse generation." Then those who gladly received his word were baptized; and that day about three thousand souls were added to them.

Ethiopian Baptized

Acts 8:36-39 Now as they went down the road, they came to some water. And the eunuch said, "See, here is water. What hinders me from being baptized?"

Then Philip said, "If you believe with all your heart, you may."

And he answered and said, "I believe that Jesus Christ is the Son of God."

So he commanded the chariot to stand still. And both Philip and the eunuch went down into the water, and he baptized him. Now when they came up out of the water, the Spirit of the Lord caught Philip away, so that the eunuch saw him no more; and he went on his way rejoicing.

Pattern Continued
  ➤ *A Privilege*

Acts 10:47,48 Can anyone forbid water, that these should not be baptized who have received the Holy Spirit just as we have? And he commanded them to be baptized in the name of the Lord. Then they asked him to stay a few days.

All through the New Testament people were saved and then were immediately baptized.

  ➤ *People of Samaria*

Acts 8:12 But when they believed Philip as he preached the things concerning the kingdom of God and the name of Jesus Christ, both men and women were baptized.

  ➤ *Lydia*

Acts 16:15 And when she and her household were baptized, she begged us, saying, "If you have judged me to be faithful to the Lord, come to my house and stay."

  ➤ *The Jailer*

Acts 16:33 And he took them the same hour of the night and washed their stripes. And immediately he and all his family were baptized.

➤ *Ruler of Synagogue*

Acts 18:8 Then Crispus, the ruler of the synagogue, believed on the Lord with all his household. And many of the Corinthians, hearing, believed and were baptized.

➤ *The Corinthians*

Acts 19:5 When they heard this, they were baptized in the name of the Lord Jesus.

➤ *Ananias Commanded Paul*

Acts 22:16   'And now why are you waiting? Arise and be baptized, and wash away your sins, calling on the name of the Lord.'

QUESTIONS FOR REVIEW

1. What are the two important statements Jesus made about the church in Matthew 16:18?

2. Describe the distinctions between the baptism by the Holy Spirit into Jesus and the baptism by Jesus into the Holy Spirit.

3 Why is water baptism important?

SECTION TWO

MINISTRIES
IN THE BOOK OF ACTS

Lesson Seven

Peter the Reed

PETER AS HE WALKED WITH JESUS

We are given more incidents in the life of Peter than we are of any of the other disciples. Peter was the leader of the disciples. His name is always at the first of the list. He was the one that spoke out most often. He was bold, confident, courageous, frank, impulsive, and strong. He was subject to change and he sometimes seemed forward and rash.

Met Jesus

Peter may have been a follower of John the Baptist. We know that it was the Baptist who pointed him to Jesus as the Lamb of God. The first mention of Peter in the Bible is also the time when he was renamed by Jesus. His first name was Simon which some have said means a reed. A reed by its very nature is tossed to and fro in the wind. Jesus immediately renamed him Peter which means a rock, although Jesus called him Simon or Peter interchangeably throughout the gospels.

John 1:35-42   Again, the next day, John stood with two of his disciples. And I as He walked, he said, "Behold the Lamb of God!" The two disciples heard him speak, and they followed Jesus.

Then Jesus turned, and seeing them following, said to them, "What do you seek?"

They said to Him, "Rabbi" (which is to say, when translated, Teacher), "where are You staying?"

He said to them, "Come and see."

They came and saw where He was staying, and remained with Him that day (now it was about the tenth hour). One of the two who heard John speak, and followed Him, was Andrew, Simon Peter's brother.

He first found his own brother Simon, and said to him, "We have found the Messiah" (which is translated, the Christ). And he brought him to Jesus.

Name Changed to Peter

Now when Jesus looked at him, He said, "You are Simon the son of Jonah. You shall be called Cephas" (which is translated, A Stone).

Miraculous Catch of Fish

Sometimes when reading of the miraculous things that happened in the Bible, we enjoy the miracles so much that we forget to look for the resulting change in the lives of the people involved.

Jesus used Peter's boat as a "teaching platform." Peter willingly gave Him the use of the boat and of himself since he was the one who moved the boat a little from the shore. When Jesus finished teaching, He said to Peter, "Put out into deep water and let down the nets for a catch."

Peter had a choice. He could do as Jesus said, even though it made no sense on the human level, or he could refuse. Peter chose to obey.

Peter Obeyed

Because Peter obeyed, he saw the supernatural power of God. He realized his own sinful condition and he recognized Jesus as Lord. Immediately, he was called by Jesus and left everything to follow Him.

Luke 5:1-11 Now so it was, as the multitude pressed about Him to hear the word of God, that He stood by the Lake of Gennesaret, and saw two boats standing by the lake; but the fishermen had gone from them and were washing their nets.

Then He got into one of the boats, which was Simon's, and asked him to put out a little from the land. And He sat down and taught the multitudes from the boat.

Now when He had stopped speaking, He said to Simon, "Launch out into the deep and let down your nets for a catch."

But Simon answered and said to Him, "Master, we have toiled all night and caught nothing; nevertheless at Your word I will let down the net."

➤ *Blessings Came*

vs. 6,7 And when they had done this, they caught a great number of fish, and their net was breaking. So they signaled to their partners in the other boat to come and help them. And they came and filled both the boats, so that they began to sink.

➤ *Peter Called by Jesus*

vs. 8-11 When Simon Peter saw it, he fell down at Jesus' knees, saying, "Depart from me, for I am a sinful man, O Lord!" For he and all who were with him were astonished at the catch of fish which they had taken; and so also were James and John, the sons of Zebedee, who were partners with Simon.

And Jesus said to Simon, "Do not be afraid. From now on you will catch men." So when they had brought their boats to land, they forsook all and followed Him.

Peter Walked on Water

When Jesus was walking on the water toward the boat, the disciples saw Him and were afraid. They did not know it was Jesus, but thought instead He was a ghost. The first reaction of many believers is fear when they see the supernatural manifestations of God.

Jesus called out "It is I. Don't be afraid." Only Peter responded. He climbed out of the boat. He walked on the water and then when Peter looked around at the circumstances, he began to doubt and to sink.

Jesus did chide him for his unbelief but it would be well to remember that Peter did walk on the water. Peter was willing to move out into the dangerous situation. Peter was obedient. Jesus said, "Come" and Peter went!

Matthew 14:25-33 Now in the fourth watch of the night Jesus went to them, walking on the sea. And when the disciples saw Him walking on the sea, they were troubled, saying, "It is a ghost!" And they cried out for fear.

But immediately Jesus spoke to them, saying, "Be of good cheer! It is I; do not be afraid."

And Peter answered Him and said, "Lord, if it is You, command me to come to You on the water."

So He said, "Come."

And when Peter had come down out of the boat, he walked on the water to go to Jesus. But when he saw that the wind was boisterous, he was afraid; and beginning to sink he cried out, saying, "Lord, save me!"

And immediately Jesus stretched out His hand and caught him, and said to him, "O you of little faith, why did you doubt?"

And when they got into the boat, the wind ceased. Then those who were in the boat came and worshiped Him, saying, "Truly You are the Son of God."

Peter Remained

Many of the disciples that followed Jesus had found His way too hard and had turned back, but not Peter!

John 6:67-69 Then Jesus said to the twelve, "Do you also want to go away?"

Then Simon Peter answered Him, "Lord, to whom shall we go? You have the words of eternal life. Also we have come to believe and know that You are the Christ, the Son of the living God."

"You Are Christ"

Peter was the main spokesman for the Twelve. It was he that answered Jesus on several occasions. It was Peter that confessed that the man they had received as a prophet was the Messiah.

Matthew 16:13-20 When Jesus came into the region of Caesarea Philippi, He asked His disciples, saying, "Who do men say that I, the Son of Man, am?"

So they said, "Some say John the Baptist, some Elijah, and others Jeremiah or one of the prophets."

He said to them, "But who do you say that I am?"

And Simon Peter answered and said, "You are the Christ, the Son of the living God."

Jesus answered and said to him, "Blessed are you, Simon Bar-Jonah, for flesh and blood has not revealed this to you, but My Father who is in heaven.

And I also say to you that you are Peter, and on this rock I will build My church, and the gates of Hades shall not prevail against it. And I will give you the keys of the kingdom of heaven, and whatever you bind on earth will be bound in heaven, and whatever you loose on

earth will be loosed in heaven." Then He commanded His disciples that they should tell no one that He was Jesus the Christ.

Notice that Jesus did not say, "You are Peter and on you I will build my church." Jesus said you are Peter (not the reed Simon that blows in the wind, but Peter the little rock) and on this big rock of revelation evidenced by Peter's confession that Jesus was the Christ, He would build His church.

When Jesus continued, He told them that He would give them the keys of the kingdom and the power of binding and loosing. He was speaking to all the disciples as His believers.

This power and authority was not given only to Peter. It was to be given to all believers to fulfill His Great Commission.

Once Rebuked Jesus

Peter understood who Jesus was by the Spirit. Jesus said this was not revealed to him by man, but by the Father in heaven. But when Jesus began to explain what He was going to suffer, that He would be killed and that He would be raised to life. Peter moved into the area of the soul. His lack of understanding and his love for Jesus caused him to try to prevent what he considered to be evil.

Jesus then had to rebuke him.

Matthew 16:21-23 From that time Jesus began to show to His disciples that He must go to Jerusalem, and suffer many things from the elders and chief priests and scribes, and be killed, and be raised again the third day. Then Peter took Him aside and began to rebuke Him, saying, "Far be it from You, Lord; this shall not happen to You!"

But He turned and said to Peter, "Get behind Me, Satan! You are an offense to Me, for you are not mindful of the things of God, but the things of men."

Man of Faith

Peter was a man of faith. When Jesus was going to heal Jairus' daughter he would not let anyone come with him except Peter, James and John.

Jesus knew that He must be surrounded by faith and not doubt.

Mark 5:35-42 While He was still speaking, some came from the ruler of the synagogue's house who said, "Your daughter is dead. Why trouble the Teacher any further?"

As soon as Jesus heard the word that was spoken, He said to the ruler of the synagogue, "Do not be afraid; only believe." And He permitted no one to follow Him except Peter, James, and John the brother of James.

Then He came to the house of the ruler of the synagogue, and saw a tumult and those who wept and wailed loudly. When He came

in, He said to them, "Why make this commotion and weep? The child is not dead, but sleeping." And they laughed Him to scorn.

But when He had put them all out, He took the father and the mother of the child, and those who were with Him, and entered where the child was lying. Then He took the child by the hand, and said to her, "Talitha, cumi," which is translated, "Little girl, I say to you, arise." Immediately the girl arose and walked, for she was twelve years of age. And they were overcome with great amazement.

Witness to Transfiguration

Peter was selected from among the Twelve several times. Peter, James and John were allowed to see Jesus transformed.

Matthew 17:1-5 Now after six days Jesus took Peter, James, and John his brother, brought them up on a high mountain by themselves, and was transfigured before them. His face shone like the sun, and His clothes became as white as the light. And behold, Moses and Elijah appeared to them, talking with Him.

Then Peter answered and said to Jesus, "Lord, it is good for us to be here; if You wish, let us make here three tabernacles: one for You, one for Moses, and one for Elijah."

While he was still speaking, behold, a bright cloud overshadowed them; and suddenly a voice came out of the cloud, saying, "This is My beloved Son, in whom I am well pleased. Hear Him!"

Peter and Fish

The tax collectors came to Peter and Peter went to Jesus. Because Peter was not afraid to talk to Jesus about a problem, the problem was taken care of not only for Jesus but for himself.

Matthew 17:24-27 And when they had come to Capernaum, those who received the temple tax came to Peter and said, "Does your Teacher not pay the temple tax?"

He said, "Yes."

And when he had come into the house, Jesus anticipated him, saying, "What do you think, Simon? From whom do the kings of the earth take customs or taxes, from their own sons or from strangers?"

Peter said to Him, "From strangers."

Jesus said to him, "Then the sons are free. Nevertheless, lest we offend them, go to the sea, cast in a hook, and take the fish that comes up first. And when you have opened its mouth, you will find a piece of money; take that and give it to them for Me and you."

Again, Peter was allowed to partake in a miracle of Jesus. Jesus told him to catch a fish and the first one would have a coin in its mouth and he could pay the taxes from that.

Again, Jesus asked Peter to do the unreasonable thing and Peter obeyed and was blessed.

PETER FAILED!

The Problem

➢ *Overconfident*

Jesus called Simon out before the others and warned him of what was about to happen.

Luke 22:31-34 And the Lord said, "Simon, Simon! Indeed, Satan has asked for you, that he may sift you as wheat. But I have prayed for you, that your faith should not fail; and when you have returned to Me, strengthen your brethren."

But he said to Him, "Lord, I am ready to go with You, both to prison and to death."

Then He said, "I tell you, Peter, the rooster will not crow this day before you will deny three times that you know Me."

Matthew 26:31-35 Then Jesus said to them, "All of you will be made to stumble because of Me this night, for it is written: 'I will strike the Shepherd, and the sheep of the flock will be scattered.' But after I have been raised, I will go before you to Galilee."

➢ *Boastful*

Peter answered and said to Him, "Even if all are made to stumble because of You, I will never be made to stumble."

Jesus said to him, "Assuredly, I say to you that this night, before the rooster crows, you will deny Me three times."

Peter said to Him, "Even if I have to die with You, I will not deny You!" And so said all the disciples.

Peter at Gethsemane
➢ *Selected by Jesus*

Simon was chosen along with James and John to go on with Jesus in the Garden and to wait and watch with Him. Jesus even warned him again that he was going to fail if he did not spend this time in prayer, but Simon slept anyway.

Matthew 26:36-46 Then Jesus came with them to a place called Gethsemane, and said to the disciples, "Sit here while I go and pray over there." And He took with Him Peter and the two sons of Zebedee, and He began to be sorrowful and deeply distressed. Then He said to them, "My soul is exceedingly sorrowful, even to death. Stay here and watch with Me." He went a little farther and fell on His face, and prayed, saying, "O My Father, if it is possible, let this cup pass from Me; nevertheless, not as I will, but as You will."

Then He came to the disciples and found them asleep, and said to Peter, "What, could you not watch with Me one hour? Watch and pray, lest you enter into temptation. The spirit indeed is willing, but the flesh is weak."

He went away again a second time and prayed, saying, "O My Father, if this cup cannot pass away from Me unless I drink it, Your will be done." And He came and found them asleep again,

for their eyes were heavy. So He left them, went away again, and prayed the third time, saying the same words.

Then He came to His disciples and said to them, "Are you still sleeping and resting? Behold, the hour is at hand, and the Son of Man is being betrayed into the hands of sinners. Rise, let us be going. See, he who betrays Me is at hand."

➢ *Severed Malchus' Ear*

Peter was willing to die fighting for Jesus because that was something he could understand. That was a work of the flesh.

John 18:10 Then Simon Peter, having a sword, drew it and struck the high priest's servant, and cut off his right ear. The servant's name was Malchus.

Peter Denied Jesus

Matthew 26:56b-58 Then all the disciples forsook Him and fled. And those who had laid hold of Jesus led Him away to Caiaphas the high priest, where the scribes and the elders were assembled. But Peter followed Him at a distance to the high priest's courtyard. And he went in and sat with the servants to see the end.

Mark 14:66-72 Now as Peter was below in the courtyard, one of the servant girls of the high priest came. And when she saw Peter warming himself, she looked at him and said, "You also were with Jesus of Nazareth."

But he denied it, saying, "I neither know nor understand what you are saying." And he went out on the porch, and a rooster crowed.

And the servant girl saw him again, and began to say to those who stood by, "This is one of them." But he denied it again.

And a little later those who stood by said to Peter again, "Surely you are one of them; for you are a Galilean, and your speech shows it."

But he began to curse and swear, "I do not know this Man of whom you speak!"

And a second time the rooster crowed. And Peter called to mind the word that Jesus had said to him, "Before the rooster crows twice, you will deny Me three times." And when he thought about it, he wept.

The only books that Peter wrote in the New Testament were First and Second Peter. According to some scholars, the Gospel of Mark was written at least in part under the direction of Peter. In this gospel, the story of Peter's denial is certainly written plainly for all to read.

It would be terrible if the story of Peter ended here. He would be considered in history as just a little better than Judas. But Peter's life is always a study in the mighty power of God to forgive and to change lives.

MORNING OF THE RESURRECTION

Mary Magdalene came to the tomb and saw that the stone had been rolled away and she immediately ran to John and Peter. They ran back to the tomb.

John 20:-10 On the first day of the week Mary Magdalene came to the tomb early, while it was still dark, and saw that the stone had been taken away from the tomb. Then she ran and came to Simon Peter, and to the other disciple, whom Jesus loved, and said to them, "They have taken away the Lord out of the tomb, and we do not know where they have laid Him."

Peter therefore went out, and the other disciple, and were going to the tomb. So they both ran together, and the other disciple outran Peter and came to the tomb first. And he, stooping down and looking in, saw the linen cloths lying there; yet he did not go in. Then Simon Peter came, following him, and went into the tomb; and he saw the linen cloths lying there, and the handkerchief that had been around His head, not lying with the linen cloths, but folded together in a place by itself. Then the other disciple, who came to the tomb first, went in also; and he saw and believed. For as yet they did not know the Scripture, that He must rise again from the dead. Then the disciples went away again to their own homes.

According to Mark, an angel appeared to the women at the tomb and told them to tell the disciples and Peter that Jesus was going to Galilee and they would see Him there, just as Jesus had said.

Mark 16:7 "But go and tell His disciples-and Peter-that He is going before you into Galilee; there you will see Him, as He said to you."

Peter Saw Risen Lord

Peter was the first of the disciples to see Jesus after His resurrection. The two men on the road to Emmaus walked and talked with Jesus but did not recognize Him until He broke bread with them. They came back to Jerusalem to tell the disciples:

Luke 24:34 Saying, "The Lord is risen indeed, and has appeared to Simon!"

1 Corinthians 15:3-5 For I delivered to you first of all that which I also received: that Christ died for our sins according to the Scriptures, and that He was buried, and that He rose again the third day according to the Scriptures, and that He was seen by Cephas, then by the twelve.

Threefold Confession

Jesus appeared to the disciples the third time. This time He addressed Peter directly.

John 21:15-19 So when they had eaten breakfast, Jesus said to Simon Peter, "Simon, son of Jonah, do you love Me more than these?"

He said to Him, "Yes, Lord; You know that I love You."

He said to him, "Feed My lambs."

He said to him again a second time, "Simon, son of Jonah, do you love Me?"

He said to Him, "Yes, Lord; You know that I love You."

He said to him, "Tend My sheep."

He said to him the third time, "Simon, son of Jonah, do you love Me?"

Peter was grieved because He said to him the third time, "Do you love Me?" And he said to Him, "Lord, You know all things; You know that I love You."

Jesus said to him, "Feed My sheep. Most assuredly, I say to you, when you were younger, you girded yourself and walked where you wished; but when you are old, you will stretch out your hands, and another will gird you and carry you where you do not wish." This He spoke, signifying by what death he would glorify God. And when He had spoken this, He said to him, "Follow Me."

Peter had denied Jesus three times and now was completely restored by telling Jesus three times that he loved Him.

Summary

Peter was a normal working man, a fisherman, when Jesus came into his life. By walking with Jesus on a daily basis for three years, he was trained for ministry. The same can be true for any believer today. The secret in Peter's life is commitment. Peter committed his life totally to Jesus. He committed his work, his friends, his time, everything to Jesus. The Lord can use a committed vessel today. He wants to use each one of us!

QUESTIONS FOR REVIEW

1. What was the supernatural revelation which Peter received concerning the person of Jesus?

2. Give an example of Peter's faith.

3. Give examples of Peter's failures.

4. What were the three commands that Jesus gave to Peter as Peter assured Jesus that he loved Him.

Peter the Rock

BEGINNING OF PETER'S MINISTRY

Peter became strong in faith. There was never a wavering of faith in him after the time of his denial of Jesus. When he received the power of the Holy Spirit at Pentecost, he was a different person. He was truly Peter, the rock.

Peter's ministry was a pattern of what God wants us to do today. It is interesting to note that first, Peter witnessed in Jerusalem and Judea, then to Samaria.

Acts 1:8 But you shall receive power when the Holy Spirit has come upon you; and you shall be witnesses to Me in Jerusalem, and in all Judea and Samaria, and to the end of the earth.

Place of Ministry

Peter's ministry was more to the Jewish people than to the Gentiles.

Galatians 2:7,8 But on the contrary, when they saw that the gospel for the uncircumcised had been committed to me, as the gospel for the circumcised was to Peter (for He who worked effectively in Peter for the apostleship to the circumcised also worked effectively in me toward the Gentiles).

Just as God called Peter to a certain group of people, He has a special place of ministry for every believer. Some are called to the drug addicts, the alcoholics, the prostitutes, the homeless, the abused women, or to the professional people. Others are called to certain nations or races of people. The important thing is to find God's will for your ministry. As you do, you will experience great power and effectiveness in your ministry.

First Sermon
Acts 2:14-41

Peter was the principal speaker on the day of Pentecost.

Acts 2:14 But Peter, standing up with the eleven, raised his voice and said to them, "Men of Judea and all who dwell in Jerusalem, let this be known to you, and heed my words."

First Recorded Miracle
Acts 3:1-11

Peter as well as John was prominent in the first detailed recorded miracle performed by the apostles after the day of Pentecost. It was the healing of the lame man at the gate of the temple.

Acts 3:1-9 Now Peter and John went up together to the temple at the hour of prayer, the ninth hour. And a certain man lame from his mother's womb was carried, whom they laid daily at the gate of the temple which is called Beautiful, to ask alms from those who entered the temple; who, seeing Peter and John about to go

into the temple, asked for alms. And fixing his eyes on him, with John, Peter said, "Look at us." So he gave them his attention, expecting to receive something from them.

Then Peter said, "Silver and gold I do not have, but what I do have I give you: in the name of Jesus Christ of Nazareth, rise up and walk." And he took him by the right hand and lifted him up, and immediately his feet and ankle bones received strength. So he, leaping up, stood and walked and entered the temple with them-walking, leaping, and praising God. And all the people saw him walking and praising God.

First Persecution
Acts 4

As a result of this miracle, many were saved and their numbers grew to 5,000 men. The Jewish religious leaders threw Peter and John in jail and then the next day began to question them. Peter was the main spokesman in this time of persecution.

Acts 4:7,8 And when they had set them in the midst, they asked, "By what power or by what name have you done this?" Then Peter, filled with the Holy Spirit, said to them, "Rulers of the people and elders of Israel ..."

Peter Operated in Authority
Acts 5:1-11

Peter was used by the Holy Spirit to protect and guard the Church from sin and deception.

Acts 5:1,2 But a certain man named Ananias, with Sapphira his wife, sold a possession. And he kept back part of the proceeds, his wife also being aware of it, and brought a certain part and laid it at the apostles' feet.

Operated in Word of Knowledge

vs. 3-6 But Peter said, "Ananias, why has Satan filled your heart to lie to the Holy Spirit and keep back part of the price of the land for yourself? While it remained, was it not your own? And after it was sold, was it not in your own control? Why have you conceived this thing in your heart? You have not lied to men but to God."

Then Ananias, hearing these words, fell down and breathed his last. So great fear came upon all those who heard these things. And the young men arose and wrapped him up, carried him out, and buried him.

➤ *Gave Sapphira Opportunity*

Peter gave Sapphira the opportunity to be honest.

vs. 7-9 Now it was about three hours later when his wife came in, not knowing what had happened. And Peter answered her, "Tell me whether you sold the land for so much?"

And she said, "Yes, for so much."

Then Peter said to her, "How is it that you have agreed together to test the Spirit of the Lord? Look, the feet of those who have buried your husband are at the door, and they will carry you out."

➤ *Godly Fear Was Result*

vs. 10,11 Then immediately she fell down at his feet and breathed her last. And the young men came in and found her dead, and carrying her out, buried her by her husband. So great fear came upon all the church and upon all who heard these things.

Not all fear is bad. The fear that came on these people was because they realized the mighty power of God and that He demanded truthfulness from them. Fear and reverence for the Lord are important for God's people.

➤ *Discerning of Evil*

The church needs to be protected from evil in its midst. The Holy Spirit will warn those in charge, of evil, just as the Holy Spirit warned Peter about Ananias and Sapphira.

Peter operated in the gift of the word of knowledge. He knew about the deception of the money. No one had required that they sell the property. They must have done so and lied because they wanted a certain "position" in that body of believers. Their real sin was not in withholding some of the money, but in lying to the Holy Spirit.

It is interesting that there was three hours between the time Ananias died and his wife came in and during that time no one told her what had happened. The people must have been so awed by the power of God that they did not want to do anything that might be sin!

"Shadow Ministry"
Acts 5:12-16

The power of God flowing through Peter was so great that even his shadow had power to heal.

Acts 5:14-16 And believers were increasingly added to the Lord, multitudes of both men and women, so that they brought the sick out into the streets and laid them on beds and couches, that at least the shadow of Peter passing by might fall on some of them. Also a multitude gathered from the surrounding cities to Jerusalem, bringing sick people and those who were tormented by unclean spirits, and they were all healed.

INTERNATIONAL MINISTRY

Peter traveled and ministered in many areas outside of Jerusalem and Judea.

Samaria
Acts 8:14-25

➤ *People Received Baptism*

Acts 8:14-17 Now when the apostles who were at Jerusalem heard that Samaria had received the word of God, they sent Peter and John to them, who, when they had come down, prayed for them that they might receive the Holy Spirit. For as yet He had fallen upon none of them. They had only been baptized in the name of the Lord Jesus. Then they laid hands on them, and they received the Holy Spirit.

Peter and John laid their hands on the people and they received the baptism of the Holy Spirit.

Jesus said we were to minister first in Jerusalem (hometown) and Judea (home area), then to the Samartians (those we tend to look down on) and then to the ends of the earth.

Notice the pattern of Peter's ministry.

➤ *Evil Discerned*

When Simon the Sorcerer saw the power that was manifested through Peter's hands, he wanted to buy that power. Peter's reaction was direct and to the point.

Acts 8:20-23 But Peter said to him, "Your money perish with you, because you thought that the gift of God could be purchased with money! You have neither part nor portion in this matter, for your heart is not right in the sight of God. Repent therefore of this your wickedness, and pray God if perhaps the thought of your heart may be forgiven you. For I see that you are poisoned by bitterness and bound by iniquity."

Peter operated in the spiritual gift of distinguishing between spirits.

Lydda
Acts 9:32-35

As Peter traveled he did what he had seen Jesus do. Jesus had commissioned Peter and all of the believers to do the works that He did.

➤ *Aeneas Healed*

Peter went to visit the saints in Lydda. There he found a man named Aeneas, a paralytic who had been bedridden for eight years. "Aeneas," Peter said to him, "Arise and make your bed." Then he arose immediately. So all who dwelt at Lydda and Sharon saw him and turned to the Lord.

Joppa
Acts 9:36-43

➤ *Dorcas Resurrected*

Peter had been there when Jesus raised Jairus' daughter from the dead. When Peter felt God would have him raise Dorcas from the dead, he knew what Jesus would do and he did the same.

Acts 9:36-42 At Joppa there was a certain disciple named Tabitha, which is translated Dorcas. This woman was full of good works and charitable deeds which she did. But it happened in those days that she became sick and died. When they had washed her, they laid her in an upper room. And since Lydda was near Joppa, and the disciples had heard that Peter was there, they sent two men to him, imploring him not to delay in coming to them. Then Peter arose and went with them. When he had come, they brought him to the upper room. And all the widows stood by him weeping, showing the tunics and garments which Dorcas had made while she was with them.

But Peter put them all out, and knelt down and prayed. And turning to the body he said, "Tabitha, arise." And she opened her eyes, and when she saw Peter she sat up. Then he gave her his hand and lifted her up; and when he had called the saints and widows, he presented her alive. And it became known throughout all Joppa, and many believed on the Lord.

Remember how Jesus had sent everyone out of the room except the parents and the three disciples? Jesus had removed those who would not believe. Peter did the same.

Faith functions in compassion, but never in the soulish realm of sympathy. Acting in sympathy, we would raise everyone from the dead. However, it is not God's will for every person to be raised from the dead. In this area of faith it is very important to hear a clear word from the Lord. Remember that Jesus said He only did what He saw His Father doing. The dead are only raised when one receives a supernatural word of wisdom, thereby releasing the gift of faith.

John 5:19 Then Jesus answered and said to them, "Most assuredly, I say to you, the Son can do nothing of Himself, but what He sees the Father do; for whatever He does, the Son also does in like manner."

Caesarea
Acts 10

➤ *The Vision*

Peter's main call was to the Jewish people. He was also the one that God used to open the door to the Gentile world.

The vision that God gave Peter and the teaching that came through it, is very special, because through it we see God's faithfulness to teach us those things we need to know or to understand so that we can do His will.

As a Jew, Peter was prejudiced against the Gentiles. He would never have willingly allowed a Gentile to come into his home and he would never have gone into their home, but God had a special mission for Peter and this prejudice had to be broken.

Acts 10:10-23 Then he became very hungry and wanted to eat; but while they made ready, he fell into a trance and saw heaven opened and an object like a great sheet bound at the four corners, descending to him and let down to the earth. In it were all kinds of four-footed animals of the earth, wild beasts, creeping things, and birds of the air.

And a voice came to him, "Rise, Peter; kill and eat."

But Peter said, "Not so, Lord! For I have never eaten anything common or unclean."

And a voice spoke to him again the second time, "What God has cleansed you must not call common." This was done three times. And the object was taken up into heaven again. Now while Peter wondered within himself what this vision which he had seen

meant, behold, the men who had been sent from Cornelius had made inquiry for Simon's house, and stood before the gate. And they called and asked whether Simon, whose surname was Peter, was lodging there.

While Peter thought about the vision, the Spirit said to him, "Behold, three men are seeking you. Arise therefore, go down and go with them, doubting nothing; for I have sent them."

Then Peter went down to the men who had been sent to him from Cornelius, and said, "Yes, I am he whom you seek. For what reason have you come?"

And they said, "Cornelius the centurion, a just man, one who fears God and has a good reputation among all the nation of the Jews, was divinely instructed by a holy angel to summon you to his house, and to hear words from you." Then he invited them in and lodged them. On the next day Peter went away with them, and some brethren from Joppa accompanied him.

➤ *Gentiles Received Holy Spirit*

Acts 10:24,25,27,28 And the following day they entered Caesarea. Now Cornelius was waiting for them, and had called together his relatives and close friends. As Peter was coming in, Cornelius met him and fell down at his feet and worshiped him.

And as he talked with him, he went in and found many who had come together. Then he said to them, "You know how unlawful it is for a Jewish man to keep company with or go to one of another nation. But God has shown me that I should not call any man common or unclean."

They continued talking and Peter began to explain to them who Jesus really was.

Acts 10:43-46a To Him all the prophets witness that, through His name, whoever believes in Him will receive remission of sins. While Peter was still speaking these words, the Holy Spirit fell upon all those who heard the word. And those of the circumcision who believed were astonished, as many as came with Peter, because the gift of the Holy Spirit had been poured out on the Gentiles also. For they heard them speak with tongues and magnify God.

Peter's Report
Acts 11:1-18

Peter had broken from man's tradition. He had gone into the home of the uncircumcised and eaten with them.

Peter told the other apostles what had happened, about the vision he had received, about the men coming to him, and how he had gone to them and they had received salvation and the baptism of the Holy Spirit. He concluded,

Acts 11:17,18 "If therefore God gave them the same gift as He gave us when we believed on the Lord Jesus Christ, who was I that I could withstand God?"

When they heard these things they became silent; and they glorified God, saying, "Then God has also granted to the Gentiles repentance to life."

This is the first time the apostles realized that salvation was for all the world, not just for all the Jews living around the world.

PETER'S MIRACULOUS DELIVERANCE FROM JAIL

Acts 12:1-19
Impending Death

Often Jesus had called Peter, James and John apart from the others. King Herod had James put to death with a sword and then he had Peter imprisoned. Peter must have felt there was a good chance that he was going to die also.

Acts 12:1-16 Now about that time Herod the king stretched out his hand to harass some from the church. Then he killed James the brother of John with the sword. And because he saw that it pleased the Jews, he proceeded further to seize Peter also. Now it was during the Days of Unleavened Bread. So when he had apprehended him, he put him in prison, and delivered him to four squads of soldiers to keep him, intending to bring him before the people after Passover.

Church Intercedes

vs. 5-7 Peter was therefore kept in prison, but constant prayer was offered to God for him by the church. And when Herod was about to bring him out, that night Peter was sleeping, bound with two chains between two soldiers; and the guards before the door were keeping the prison.

Now behold, an angel of the Lord stood by him, and a light shone in the prison; and he struck Peter on the side and raised him up, saying, "Arise quickly!" And his chains fell off his hands.

Peter Released

vs. 8-11 Then the angel said to him, "Gird yourself and tie on your sandals"; and so he did. And he said to him, "Put on your garment and follow me." So he went out and followed him, and did not know that what was done by the angel was real, but thought he was seeing a vision. When they were past the first and the second guard posts, they came to the iron gate that leads to the city, which opened to them of its own accord; and they went out and went down one street, and immediately the angel departed from him.

And when Peter had come to himself, he said, "Now I know for certain that the Lord has sent His angel, and has delivered me from the hand of Herod and from all the expectation of the Jewish people."

Others Prayed

v. 12 So, when he had considered this, he came to the house of Mary, the mother of John whose surname was Mark, where many were gathered together praying.

Prayers Answered

vs. 13,14 And as Peter knocked at the door of the gate, a girl named Rhoda came to answer. When she recognized Peter's

voice, because of her gladness she did not open the gate, but ran in and announced that Peter stood before the gate.

Disbelief

vs. 15,16 But they said to her, "You are beside yourself!" Yet she kept insisting that it was so. So they said, "It is his angel." Now Peter continued knocking; and when they opened the door and saw him, they were astonished.

Sometimes it is easy to miss the real message God has for us in telling an incident. Yes, the people were shocked when Peter was actually set free from the prison and came to their prayer meeting. We could say, "Where was their real faith?" But what we should understand is their concern for Peter and the sacrifice of time they made to come together and pray. If they had not prayed it is very possible that Peter would have been killed just like James.

King Herod Dies
Acts 12:19-23

King Herod had killed James. He had planned to kill Peter. He had killed the guards that "let" Peter go. But King Herod was soon to die himself.

Acts 12:21-24 So on a set day Herod, arrayed in royal apparel, sat on his throne and gave an oration to them. And the people kept shouting, "The voice of a god and not of a man!"

Then immediately an angel of the Lord struck him, because he did not give glory to God. And he was eaten by worms and died. But the word of God grew and multiplied.

PETER'S DEATH

We are told nothing of Peter's death in the scripture. We know that Jesus prophesied concerning it.

John 21:18,19 "Most assuredly, I say to you, when you were younger, you girded yourself and walked where you wished; but when you are old, you will stretch out your hands, and another will gird you and carry you where you do not wish."

This He spoke, signifying by what death he would glorify God. And when He had spoken this, He said to him, "Follow Me."

According to some traditions, Peter went to Rome directly following his miraculous release from prison and he was crucified there under Nero. It is also tradition that he refused to die like Jesus and requested that he be crucified head down. There is nothing to substantiate this in scripture. We have several accounts of Paul being in Rome but he never mentions anything about Peter being there or having been there.

Summary

The study of Peter's life is a study of miracles. The first miracle is the change in the life of Peter from the time he first started to follow Jesus, denied Jesus at His trial, received the baptism of the Holy Spirit and immediately became bold, fearing no man, and not even fearing death.

He saw Jesus work miracles, and he worked miracles. The anointing was so strong upon Peter at times that when his shadow came across people, they were healed. He exposed sin in the church and people fell dead. Peter raised Dorcas from the dead. He was in prison facing death and God sent an angel to set him free. Peter walked in the supernatural miraculous power of a living God, and we can do the same!

QUESTIONS FOR REVIEW

1. What have you learned from Peter's life after the baptism of the Holy Spirit that has meaning in your life today?

2. When Ananias and Sapphira lied to the Lord they were immediately slain. Why do you think this same thing is not happening in churches today ?

3. Why are the events that happened at Caesarea important to us today?

Lesson Nine

To Die Is Gain

The apostle Paul when faced with death said, **For to me, to live is Christ and to die is gain** (Philippians 1:21).

Through the life of Stephen we learn how a believer is to face persecution and death.

STEPHEN

Acts 6,8,7
Stephen, One of the Deacons

We know that Stephen was a man of good reputation, full of the Holy Spirit and full wisdom because these were the qualifications of a deacon.

Acts 6:3 Therefore, brethren, seek out from among you seven men of good reputation, full of the Holy Spirit and wisdom, whom we may appoint over this business ...

Immediately after he was chosen as a deacon he began to do wonders and miraculous signs among the people.

➢ *Did Miracles*

Acts 6:8-15 And Stephen, full of faith and power, did great wonders and signs among the people.

➢ *Faced Opposition*

v.9 Then there arose some from what is called the Synagogue of the Freedmen (Cyrenians, Alexandrians, and those from Cilicia and Asia),disputing with Stephen.

➢ *Had God's Wisdom*

vs.10 And they were not able to resist the wisdom and the Spirit by which he spoke.

➢ *Was Lied About*

v.11 Then they secretly induced men to say, "We have heard him speak blasphemous words against Moses and God."

➢ *Falsely Accused*

vs.12-14 And they stirred up the people, the elders, and the scribes; and they came upon him, seized him, and brought him to the council. They also set up false witnesses who said, "This man does not cease to speak blasphemous words against this holy place and the law; for we have heard him say that this Jesus of Nazareth will destroy this place and change the customs which Moses delivered to us."

➢ *Radiated God's Glory*

v. 15 And all who sat in the council, looking steadfastly at him, saw his face as the face of an angel.

Events of Stephen's Death

> *Preached Gospel*

The High Priest asked Stephen if the accusations were true and Stephen took this opportunity to preach the gospel. Stephen started with Abraham and continued on to the coming of the Messiah and even accused the religious leaders of killing Him. He ended the sermon with bold, righteous anger.

Acts 7:51-53 You stiffnecked and uncircumcised in heart and ears! You always resist the Holy Spirit; as your fathers did, so do you. Which of the prophets did your fathers not persecute? And they killed those who foretold the coming of the Just One, of whom you now have become the betrayers and murderers, who have received the law by the direction of angels and have not kept it.

Jesus had told the disciples they were not to take thought of how they would answer, and Stephen is a wonderful example of this. He allowed the Holy Spirit to flow through him and to say the things that should be said.

> *Aroused Their Anger*

The Sanhedrin and the High Priest were so mad they were gnashing their teeth.

Acts 7:54-60 When they heard these things they were cut to the heart, and they gnashed at him with their teeth.

> *Stephen Stayed in Spirit*

vs. 55,56 But he, being full of the Holy Spirit, gazed into heaven and saw the glory of God, and Jesus standing at the right hand of God, and said, "Look! I see the heavens opened and the Son of Man standing at the right hand of God!"

Stephen stayed in the Spirit and looked up into heaven to see the glory of God and Jesus standing right there beside Him.

> *Leaders Refused to Listen*

vs. 57,58a Then they cried out with a loud voice, stopped their ears, and ran at him with one accord; and they cast him out of the city and stoned him.

> *Stephen Forgave Them*

vs. 60 Then he knelt down and cried out with a loud voice, "Lord, do not charge them with this sin." And when he had said this, he fell asleep.

Stephen's Martyrdom

Stephen was the first martyr and his death was the beginning of strong persecution against the early believers. His death caused the believers to scatter abroad and they preached the Word wherever they went.

Acts 8:1-3 Now Saul was consenting to his death. At that time a great persecution arose against the church which was at

Jerusalem; and they were all scattered throughout the regions of Judea and Samaria, except the apostles. And devout men carried Stephen to his burial, and made great lamentation over him. As for Saul, he made havoc of the church, entering every house, and dragging off men and women, committing them to prison.

Acts 11:19-21 Now those who were scattered after the persecution that arose over Stephen traveled as far as Phoenicia, Cyprus, and Antioch, preaching the word to no one but the Jews only. But some of them were men from Cyprus and Cyrene, who, when they had come to Antioch, spoke to the Hellenists, preaching the Lord Jesus. And the hand of the Lord was with them, and a great number believed and turned to the Lord.

> *Witness to Saul*

Stephen's death was a witness to the man God had called to be a witness for Him to the Gentile nations.

Acts 22:20 And when the blood of Your martyr Stephen was shed, I also was standing by consenting to his death, and guarding the clothes of those who were killing him.

Saul saw Stephen's face enraptured with the Glory of God as he was martyred.

By his death, Stephen became the seed to the great harvest of souls through Paul's ministry.

Summary

Stephen was not an apostle and yet he worked miracles. Miracles were not limited to the apostles or others in the fivefold ministry. Just as the miracles brought opposition in Stephen's life, the operation of signs and wonders will bring confrontation with religious leaders and unbelievers today.

Stephen was so full of the Holy Spirit and of His wisdom that when the religious leaders tried to defend their beliefs by arguing, they could not stand against Stephen's wisdom and the Spirit of God within him.

For all believers today, Stephen is a pattern of faith, power and of being a fearless witness in the face of opposition and even at the threat of death.

WHY PERSECUTION COMES

Purifies, Strengthens, Brings Disbursement

The church is purified, strengthened and even disbursed for evangelism, through trials and persecutions.

Acts 14:21,22 And when they had preached the gospel to that city and made many disciples, they returned to Lystra, Iconium, and Antioch, strengthening the souls of the disciples, exhorting them to continue in the faith, and saying, "We must through many tribulations enter the kingdom of God."

Powerful Church a Threat

As we saw in the life of Stephen, when the supernatural power of the Holy Spirit begins to act, it brings persecution. In the first days of the church, this persecution came from the religious leaders. Often, it comes from the same source today.

Christianity posed a threat to the Jewish leaders. It was God's time to change from the God-ordained worship at the temple to the worship of God in spirit and truth.

Even now, God is doing new things as He is restoring His church. What God was saying and doing in His church a few years ago is not necessarily what He wants to reveal and do today. We must be willing to change with Him and not hold on to yesterday's patterns.

A powerful body of believers is still a threat to the uncommitted Christians of today. Often persecution comes from among this group.

Committed Christians are also a threat to the forces of evil that have confronted a powerless church for hundreds of years. Persecution will come from a godless society.

When every believer begins to do the works of Jesus, to perform mighty signs and wonders, thousands will be won to Jesus.

HOW TO FACE PERSECUTION

Areas of persecution are different. In some countries believers are facing imprisonment and even death. Sometimes the persecution is loss of a job or of family. Sometimes it is the loss of friends, or status in the community.

In all situations we are to react as Jesus did. When He was being crucified, He prayed for those killing Him. "Father forgive them, for they know not what they do."

Matthew 5:43-45a You have heard that it was said, 'You shall love your neighbor and hate your enemy.' But I say to you, love your enemies, bless those who curse you, do good to those who hate you, and pray for those who spitefully use you and persecute you, that you may be sons of your Father in heaven; for He makes His sun rise on the evil and on the good, and sends rain on the just and on the unjust.

Jesus had taught much about forgiveness in His ministry. Even in death, Jesus forgave those who were killing Him.

Stephen our Example
  ➢ *Forgive Persecutors*

Stephen's forgiveness at the time of his death should be a strong lesson for us to forgive! We have not been hurt to the point of death, so there is no excuse for any area of unforgiveness in our lives.

All through the history of the church, many have died a martyr's death. Jesus said,

John 15:13 Greater love has no one than this, than to lay down one's life for his friends.

> *Have Courage*

Most of us would say that we do not have the courage of Stephen. First, we must remember that Stephen was a true man of God. He was chosen as one of the seven deacons because he was a man of honest report, full of the Holy Ghost and of wisdom. There was no hidden sin in his life to "trip him up" at this time.

God gave him special gifts at the time of his trial. Even as He was facing death, God allowed him to see the glory of God. God allowed him to see Jesus.

> *God Gives Strength*

God gave Stephen the strength, and the words to face persecution and death.

The early believers knew that they must obey God, not man. They would continue to teach about the resurrected Jesus and to heal in the name of Jesus.

If the believers had been content to only pray and have fellowship together and not reach out to those around them, they probably would not have drawn the attention of the religious leaders to themselves. But they had a commission. They had been chosen to win the world to a saving knowledge of Jesus Christ.

> *Gospel Brings Controversy*

The same is true today. The world really does not care if we meet together and pray and worship God and have fellowship. However, when we begin to act as Jesus instructed us to act, then the controversy will come. We must remember not to seek, or deliberately stir up controversy, but when it does come, it provides an open door to present the gospel of Jesus Christ. We must never see it as a way of proving ourselves right. Self has no place in being a witness for Jesus.

Name Brings Persecution

Persecution came to the followers of Jesus because they proclaimed the name of Jesus and the power of His resurrection immediately after Pentecost. However, Peter was filled with the Holy Spirit and was able to answer their questions with boldness.

When threatened, commanded and even beaten, Peter and John did not back down. They went right on proclaiming the name of Jesus and the power of His resurrection.

Peter / John - Examples

➢ *Refuse Intimdation*

They refused to be intimidated.

When the religious leaders saw their courage they were astonished and confused.

Acts 4:13 Now when they saw the boldness of Peter and John, and perceived that they were uneducated and untrained men, they marveled. And they realized that they had been with Jesus.

➢ *Operate in Miracle Power*

Acts 4:16,17 Saying, "What shall we do to these men? For, indeed, that a notable miracle has been done through them is evident to all who dwell in Jerusalem, and we cannot deny it. But so that it spreads no further among the people, let us severely threaten them, that from now on they speak to no man in this name."

Expect Miraculous

They were arrested and thrown in jail, but during the night an angel of the Lord brought them out of the jail and told them to go stand in the temple courts and tell the people the full message.

When they were released from jail they did not run for safety. They went immediately to the temple courts and started preaching the same message.

They were brought before the Sanhedrin again, threatened with death and then beaten and allowed to go free but with a warning not to use the name of Jesus again.

➢ *Refused Compromise*

They refused to compromise.

Acts 5:40b-42 ... and when they had called for the apostles and beaten them, they commanded that they should not speak in the name of Jesus, and let them go.

➢ *Rejoiced*

So they departed from the presence of the council, rejoicing that they were counted worthy to suffer shame for His name. And daily in the temple, and in every house, they did not cease teaching and preaching Jesus as the Christ.

➢ *Obeyed*

We are to obey God even in the face of great persecutions.

Acts 8:3,4 As for Saul, he made havoc of the church, entering every house, and dragging off men and women, committing them to prison. Therefore those who were scattered went everywhere preaching the word.

➢ *Shook Off Dust*

Acts 13:49-52 And the word of the Lord was being spread throughout all the region. But the Jews stirred up the devout and

prominent women and the chief men of the city, raised up persecution against Paul and Barnabas, and expelled them from their region. But they shook off the dust from their feet against them, and came to Iconium. And the disciples were filled with joy and with the Holy Spirit.

> *Free from Rejection*

Why did Jesus tell the disciples to shake the dust off from their feet when they and their message was rejected?

The disciples were to go to the next city with no residue holding on to them from that rejection. To be free of a rejection we must forgive the people involved and then walk away from that situation.

Notice that they were immediately filled with joy and with the Holy Spirit.

QUESTIONS FOR REVIEW

1. Why was Stephen persecuted? What "mistake" had he made?

2. Name two causes of persecution. How should you react in time of persecution?

3. What is the result of persecution? Give an example.

Philip the Evangelist

MINISTRY OF PHILIP

The study of Philip should be one of the most encouraging studies to every believer that desires to do more for God and to be more effective in their ministry to Him.

First, Philip was full of faith and of the Holy Spirit, then he was appointed a deacon and finally he became an evangelist. We are told nothing of the transition.

God sees the desires of a person's heart. As that desire changes to be more and more like Jesus, God makes a way for those desires to be fulfilled in our lives.

A Deacon
Acts 6:1-7

Acts 6:5 And the saying pleased the whole multitude. And they chose Stephen, a man full of faith and the Holy Spirit, and Philip...

Just as in the selection of Stephen this selection as a deacon meant that Philip was a man of good reputation, full of the Holy Spirit, and wisdom.

An Evangelist

The last mention of Philip reveals his function as an evangelist. As Philip continued faithfully to serve God as a deacon, he was called into the fivefold ministry to function as an evangelist.

Acts 21:8 On the next day we who were Paul's companions departed and came to Caesarea, and entered the house of Philip the evangelist, who was one of the seven, and stayed with him.

After the martyrdom of Stephen, the persecution of Christians by the Jewish religious leaders began in earnest and they fled to all areas of the known world. This was the beginning of the first missionary movement. Believers who had fled Jerusalem, went everywhere preaching the name of Jesus and the power of His resurrection.

Acts 8:4 Therefore those who were scattered went everywhere preaching the word.

VARIETY IN MINISTRY

First to Samaria
Acts 8:4-25

Philip's ministry is an example of the thrilling variety of ministries in the Spirit-filled life.

Jesus had instructed the believers to go first to Jerusalem, then to Samaria, and then to the uttermost parts of the world. Philip was the first that we know about who obeyed the second part of this command. He went to Samaria and told the people about Christ.

Acts 8:4-8 Therefore those who were scattered went everywhere preaching the word. Then Philip went down to the city of Samaria and preached Christ to them. And the multitudes with one accord heeded the things spoken by Philip, hearing and seeing the miracles which he did. For unclean spirits, crying with a loud voice, came out of many who were possessed; and many who were paralyzed and lame were healed. And there was great joy in that city.

➤ *The Miracles*

People came to listen to this powerful preacher, because of the signs and wonders that followed his ministry.

➤ Lame were healed
➤ Miracles happened that the people could hear and see
➤ They listened to his words
➤ Great joy in the city

➤ *The Message*

The signs and wonders caught the attention of the crowds. But the message of Philip was the kingdom of God and the name of Jesus.

Acts 8:12 But when they believed Philip as he preached the things concerning the kingdom of God and the name of Jesus Christ, both men and women were baptized.

➤ *The Results*

Act 8:14-17 Now when the apostles who were at Jerusalem heard that Samaria had received the word of God, they sent Peter and John to them, who, when they had come down, prayed for them that they might receive the Holy Spirit. For as yet He had fallen upon none of them. They had only been baptized in the name of the Lord Jesus. Then they laid hands on them, and they received the Holy Spirit.

Notice that Philip did not say, "I'm a deacon. I'm supposed to distribute the food. God didn't call me to preach."

The signs were an open door to preaching the gospel and led to the salvation of many.

God's plan of evangelism has not changed. Every believer is still to do the works of Jesus, to perform signs and wonders, and to preach the good news of the kingdom of God.

AN EXAMPLE OF OBEDIENCE

Acts 8:26-40

An angel appeared to Philip and told him to go south. Philip walked in the miraculous. Philip did not wait for a total picture of what he was to do. An angel appeared and said go south and Philip obeyed and went. The angel did not tell him what he was to do when he got there.

Acts 8:26 Now an angel of the Lord spoke to Philip, saying, "Arise and go toward the south along the road which goes down from Jerusalem to Gaza." This is desert.

Acts 8:27,28 So he arose and went. And behold, a man of Ethiopia, a eunuch of great authority under Candace the queen of the Ethiopians, who had charge of all her treasury, and had come to Jerusalem to worship, was returning. And sitting in his chariot, he was reading Isaiah the prophet.

We too must be quick to obey God, even if we do not understand why we are going. In this story, we also see that God's timing is very important. If Philip had waited, he would have missed this opportunity.

Ministered to Ethiopian

When the chariot with the Ethiopian came by, the Spirit said, "stay near it." Still we have no record of Philip receiving a clear picture of what was going to happen. He was only told what to do and he obeyed.

Acts 8:29 Then the Spirit said to Philip, "Go near and overtake this chariot."

Acts 8:30 So Philip ran to him, and heard him reading the prophet Isaiah, and said, "Do you understand what you are reading?"

Finally, as Philip heard the man reading from Isaiah he knew what he was to do.

Acts 8:35 Then Philip opened his mouth, and beginning at this Scripture, preached Jesus to him.

Water Baptism Important

Acts 8:36-38 Now as they went down the road, they came to some water. And the eunuch said, "See, here is water. What hinders me from being baptized?"

Then Philip said, "If you believe with all your heart, you may."

And he answered and said, "I believe that Jesus Christ is the Son of God." So he commanded the chariot to stand still. And both Philip and the eunuch went down into the water, and he baptized him.

Water baptism is a testimony of our identification with Jesus in His death, burial and resurrection. It is a picture of the death of our "old self" and the resurrection of the "new creation."

Galatians 2:20 I have been crucified with Christ; it is no longer I who live, but Christ lives in me; and the life which I now live in

the flesh I live by faith in the Son of God, who loved me and gave Himself for me.

Philip Transported

Acts 8:39 Now when they came up out of the water, the Spirit of the Lord caught Philip away, so that the eunuch saw him no more; and he went on his way rejoicing.

From being with the Ethiopian, Philip appeared at Azotus. He started where he had left off and went on preaching the gospel.

Acts 8:40 But Philip was found at Azotus. And passing through, he preached in all the cities till he came to Caesarea.

PATTERN OF NEW TESTAMENT MINISTRY

Service

Philip is an example of the pattern of every believer who wants to flow in New Testament ministry. First he was obedient in a servant-like position. Being a deacon was a position of service. Philip was a fulfillment of Jesus' teaching on being a servant.

John 13:14-16 If I then, your Lord and Teacher, have washed your feet, you also ought to wash one another's feet. For I have given you an example, that you should do as I have done to you. Most assuredly, I say to you, a servant is not greater than his master; nor is he who is sent greater than he who sent him.

Signs and Wonders

We are to minister in signs, wonders and miracles. We are to minister deliverance to the oppressed.

Acts 8:6-8 And the multitudes with one accord heeded the things spoken by Philip, hearing and seeing the miracles which he did. For unclean spirits, crying with a loud voice, came out of many who were possessed; and many who were paralyzed and lame were healed. And there was great joy in that city.

Build Faith

The signs and wonders will release faith for salvation.

The new believers are to be baptized in water as a testimony of their total identification with Jesus Christ.

Acts 8:36 Now as they went down the road, they came to some water. And the eunuch said, "See, here is water. What hinders me from being baptized?"

Acts 10:47 Can anyone forbid water, that these should not be baptized who have received the Holy Spirit just as we have?

Baptized in Holy Spirit

It is important that all believers receive the baptism in the Holy Spirit. With this new power, they too will become miracle working witnesses for Jesus Christ.

Team Ministry

When the apostles heard that the Samaritans had accepted Jesus they came to help. Philip recognized the need for team ministry. He knew that foundations needed to be laid in Samaria by the ministry of the apostolic team. He did not function by himself, but was submitted to the eldership in his home church and functioned in a balanced way with the others in the fivefold ministry.

TWENTY YEARS LATER

We are told of Philip one more time twenty years later. As Paul was traveling He stayed at the home of Philip the evangelist.

Acts 21:8,9 On the next day we who were Paul's companions departed and came to Caesarea, and entered the house of Philip the evangelist, who was one of the seven, and stayed with him. Now this man had four virgin daughters who prophesied.

Summary

Philip was a layman. Then he was one of the seven selected as deacons. After that, he became an evangelist.

Philip was faithful in his obedience to God. First he served tables as a deacon. Then he moved out into miracle evangelism. Then he obeyed the angel and went to a certain road and waited until the Holy Spirit told him the next step. He lead the Ethiopian to Jesus, baptized him, and was supernaturally transported to another area.

Then we are told that twenty years later he was still an evangelist, ministering with his four daughters in Caesarea. He was still being faithful to God.

For more in-depth study of Philip the evangelist, see the **Miracle Evangelism Study Guide** by John Ezekiel.

QUESTIONS FOR REVIEW

1. What was Philip's first ministry?

2. What were the steps in Philip's life that moved him from being a deacon to being an evangelist?

3. How is Philip an example for us today in finding our place in ministry?

Conversion of Saul

PAUL'S BACKGROUND

The apostle Paul had an interesting background that is revealed in his many writings in the New Testament. He was a Jew, a Roman citizen and grew up in the Greek city of Tarsus.

We know that he was reared and trained in the doctrines of Judaism because he became a Pharisee. From his writings it is clear that he had a good knowledge of the Greek culture as well as the Roman wisdom. There is a good possibility that he spoke Greek and Latin. He was a well-educated man.

Even before his conversion, he was a well-traveled person. Saul was a Jewish name, and Paul seems to be the Roman variation of that name. In Scripture he is called Saul until his conversion and Paul most of the time following that.

Because of Paul's background, he was ideally suited for God's call on his life as an apostle to the Gentiles.

We have some details of Paul's background from the following scriptures.

Jew from Tarsus

Acts 21:39 But Paul said, "I am a Jew from Tarsus, in Cilicia,

Roman Citizen

a citizen of no mean city; and I implore you, permit me to speak to the people."

Advanced in Traditions

Galatians 1:14 And I advanced in Judaism beyond many of my contemporaries in my own nation, being more exceedingly zealous for the traditions of my fathers.

Hebrew of Hebrews

Philippines 3:4b,5 If anyone else thinks he may have confidence in the flesh, I more so: circumcised the eighth day, of the stock of Israel, of the tribe of Benjamin, a Hebrew of the Hebrews; concerning the law, a Pharisee ...

Pharisee

Acts 23:6 But when Paul perceived that one part were Sadducees and the other Pharisees, he cried out in the council, "Men and brethren, I am a Pharisee, the son of a Pharisee; concerning the hope and resurrection of the dead I am being judged!"

SAUL'S PERSECUTION OF CHURCH

Acts 7:57-8:3
First Mention of Saul

The first mention of Saul was at the time of Stephen's persecution.

Acts 7:57,58 Then they cried out with a loud voice, stopped their ears, and ran at him with one accord; and they cast him out of the city and stoned him. And the witnesses laid down their clothes at the feet of a young man named Saul.

Persecution of Christians

Paul spoke in his own words of this time, how he had persecuted the Christians, hounding them to death, binding men and women and delivering them to prison.

Acts 22:4,5 I persecuted this Way to the death, binding and delivering into prisons both men and women, as also the high priest bears me witness, and all the council of the elders, from whom I also received letters to the brethren, and went to Damascus to bring in chains even those who were there to Jerusalem to be punished.

Opposed Name of Jesus

Acts 26:9-11 Indeed, I myself thought I must do many things contrary to the name of Jesus of Nazareth. This I also did in Jerusalem, and many of the saints I shut up in prison, having received authority from the chief priests; and when they were put to death, I cast my vote against them. And I punished them often in every synagogue and compelled them to blaspheme; and being exceedingly enraged against them, I persecuted them even to foreign cities.

With the authority of the High Priest, Saul imprisoned many of the saints in Jerusalem. He felt compelled to go from city to city to be sure the Christians were caught. He even used torture to try and make Christians blaspheme Jesus. He followed them to distant cities. Paul was obsessed to persecute all Christians.

Tried to Destroy Church

Galatians 1:13,14 For you have heard of my former conduct in Judaism, how I persecuted the church of God beyond measure and tried to destroy it. And I advanced in Judaism beyond many of my contemporaries in my own nation, being more exceedingly zealous for the traditions of my fathers.

Saul was doing all of this, thinking that he was serving God. He was exceedingly zealous for his Jewish religion.

SAUL MEETS JESUS

Acts 9

God had a plan for Saul's life even while he was His enemy. God saw his heart and his mistaken zeal and supernaturally revealed Himself to Saul.

Light, Voice from Heaven

Saul was on his way to Damascus to capture more Christians when a light from heaven flashed around him and he fell to the ground. Jesus spoke directly to him.

Acts 9:3-9 And as he journeyed he came near Damascus, and suddenly a light shone around him from heaven.

Then he fell to the ground, and heard a voice saying to him, "Saul, Saul, why are you persecuting Me?"

And he said, "Who are You, Lord?"

And the Lord said, "I am Jesus, whom you are persecuting. It is hard for you to kick against the goads."

So he, trembling and astonished, said, "Lord, what do You want me to do?"

And the Lord said to him, "Arise and go into the city, and you will be told what you must do." And the men who journeyed with him stood speechless, hearing a voice but seeing no one.

Then Saul arose from the ground, and when his eyes were opened he saw no one. But they led him by the hand and brought him into Damascus. And he was three days without sight, and neither ate nor drank.

Jesus asked Saul why he was persecuting Him. To persecute a believer is to persecute Jesus Himself.

Saul's encounter with Jesus was so powerful and dramatic that he was on a total fast for three days.

Ananias Has Vision

What a man of God Ananias must have been. God knew that He could speak to Ananias and that he would obey Him at all costs to himself. Every Christian knew the name of Saul. They knew he was coming to Damascus to arrest them and to put them in prison.

Acts 9:10-16 Now there was a certain disciple at Damascus named Ananias; and to him the Lord said in a vision, "Ananias."

And he said, "Here I am, Lord."

So the Lord said to him, "Arise and go to the street called Straight, and inquire at the house of Judas for one called Saul of Tarsus, for behold, he is praying. And in a vision he has seen a man named Ananias coming in and putting his hand on him, so that he might receive his sight."

Then Ananias answered, "Lord, I have heard from many about this man, how much harm he has done to Your saints in Jerusalem. And here he has authority from the chief priests to bind all who call on Your name."

Saul a Chosen Instrument

vs. 15,16 But the Lord said to him, "Go, for he is a chosen vessel of Mine to bear My name before Gentiles, kings, and the children of Israel. For I will show him how many things he must suffer for My name's sake."

Ananias knew the voice of God. He answered immediately, "Yes, Lord." He listened to God and then he reminded God of how terrible this Saul was.

God was faithful, He gave Ananias several facts through the operation of the word of knowledge and the word of wisdom that prepared him for his ministry to Saul.

God told him:

➤ The exact house and the owner's name
➤ The name of the street
➤ The name of the man
➤ Where he was from
➤ What he was doing
➤ What he had seen
➤ Exactly what would happen

Then God told Ananias what Saul was to do in the kingdom of God and what he was to suffer. Just as Saul persecuted Jesus and His followers, so he would suffer great persecution for the name of Jesus.

Ananias Obeyed

Acts 9:17-19a And Ananias went his way and entered the house; and laying his hands on him he said, "Brother Saul, the Lord Jesus, who appeared to you on the road as you came, has sent me that you may receive your sight and be filled with the Holy Spirit." Immediately there fell from his eyes something like scales, and he received his sight at once; and he arose and was baptized. And when he had received food, he was strengthened.

Unbelief and religious tradition were instantly gone from Saul. In obedience, he was immediately baptized in water as a testimony of his total identification with Jesus Christ.

What Is Conversion?

The conversion of Saul is one of the most striking examples we have of the conversion experience.

➤ **Conversion means to make a complete change, to go from walking in one direction to abruptly changing and walking in the opposite direction.**

Paul went from darkness to light. He totally changed his whole way of living. He had become a new creation in Jesus Christ.

Paul, instantly became a powerful witness for Jesus Christ.

Acts 9:19b-22 Then Saul spent some days with the disciples at Damascus. Immediately he preached the Christ in the synagogues, that He is the Son of God.

Then all who heard were amazed, and said, "Is this not he who destroyed those who called on this name in Jerusalem, and has

come here for that purpose, so that he might bring them bound to the chief priests?" But Saul increased all the more in strength, and confounded the Jews who dwelt in Damascus, proving that this Jesus is the Christ.

Persecution of Paul

The persecution began immediately against Paul's life.

Acts 9:23-25 Now after many days were past, the Jews plotted to kill him. But their plot became known to Saul. And they watched the gates day and night, to kill him. Then the disciples took him by night and let him down through the wall in a large basket.

PAUL'S MINISTRY DEVELOPED

Time of Preparation

There were three years between Paul's conversion in Damascus and his first trip to Jerusalem. During this period of time, Paul was given the revelation and message that he preached. This truth was given to Paul by direct revelation from God.

Galatians 1:11,12,15-19 But I make known to you, brethren, that the gospel which was preached by me is not according to man. For I neither received it from man, nor was I taught it, but it came through the revelation of Jesus Christ.

But when it pleased God, who separated me from my mother's womb and called me through His grace, to reveal His Son in me, that I might preach Him among the Gentiles, I did not immediately confer with flesh and blood, nor did I go up to Jerusalem to those who were apostles before me; but I went to Arabia, and returned again to Damascus.

Then after three years I went up to Jerusalem to see Peter, and remained with him fifteen days. But I saw none of the other apostles except James, the Lord's brother.

The revelation of the Church was given to Paul during the silent years. Paul was on "hold" waiting, learning and being faithful to God.

The apostle Paul was to write thirteen books of the New Testament. After his conversion, he received the truths he would teach by direct revelation from Jesus Christ.

Sometimes God leads us in silent times and we must also be faithful at these times and listen for His voice.

Psalms 32:8 I will instruct you and teach you in the way you should go; I will guide you with My eye.

God wants to work **in** our lives in order that we will be better prepared for Him to work **through** our lives.

First Trip to Jerusalem
Acts 9:26-30

The Christians in Jerusalem did not believe it when they were told that Saul had been converted and they refused to meet with him.

Just as God had an Ananias in Damascus, He had a Barnabas in Jerusalem. He had sold everything he had and brought the money to the apostles earlier.

Acts 4:36,37 And Joses, who was also named Barnabas by the apostles (which is translated Son of Encouragement), a Levite of the country of Cyprus, having land, sold it, and brought the money and laid it at the apostles' feet.

Barnabas was mentioned a number of times in the New Testament. God used him to bring Paul to the apostles. He later traveled with Paul on some missionary journeys.

Acts 9:26-30 And when Saul had come to Jerusalem, he tried to join the disciples; but they were all afraid of him, and did not believe that he was a disciple. But Barnabas took him and brought him to the apostles. And he declared to them how he had seen the Lord on the road, and that He had spoken to him, and how he had preached boldly at Damascus in the name of Jesus. So he was with them at Jerusalem, coming in and going out.

And he spoke boldly in the name of the Lord Jesus and disputed against the Hellenists, but they attempted to kill him. When the brethren found out, they brought him down to Caesarea and sent him out to Tarsus.

A Period of Peace

After the conversion of Saul and his escape from those who were trying to kill him, the church enjoyed a time of peace.

Acts 9:31 Then the churches throughout all Judea, Galilee, and Samaria had peace and were edified. And walking in the fear of the Lord and in the comfort of the Holy Spirit, they were multiplied.

AN EXAMPLE FOR US TODAY

Started Where He Was

Paul's life is an example for us today. He started where he was and was obedient to the leading of the Lord. Paul started preaching immediately. He took a stand and let everyone know of his conversion right where he was in Damascus. After he did this, he spent three years just learning from God.

Acts 1:8 But you shall receive power when the Holy Spirit has come upon you; and you shall be witnesses to Me in Jerusalem, and in all Judea and Samaria, and to the end of the earth.

We should start exactly where we are, but be obedient to the Spirit's leading.

To be faithful in Jerusalem means to be faithful exactly where you are, where you live.

Breakthrough Came

God brought a breakthrough for Paul's ministry through others. God used Barnabas again.

To escape the persecution, some of the believers had gone to Antioch and Greeks turned to the Lord. When the apostles in Jerusalem heard of this they sent Barnabas to Antioch. Barnabas won more Greeks to the Lord and then he went in search of Paul.

Acts 11:25,26 Then Barnabas departed for Tarsus to seek Saul. And when he had found him, he brought him to Antioch. So it was that for a whole year they assembled with the church and taught a great many people. And the disciples were first called Christians in Antioch.

Promoted by God

Paul was a prophet and a teacher.

Acts 13:1-3 Now in the church that was at Antioch there were certain prophets and teachers: Barnabas, Simeon who was called Niger, Lucius of Cyrene, Manaen who had been brought up with Herod the tetrarch, and Saul. As they ministered to the Lord and fasted, the Holy Spirit said, "Now separate to Me Barnabas and Saul for the work to which I have called them." Then, having fasted and prayed, and laid hands on them, they sent them away.

Paul was chosen to be an apostle by God. The church at Antioch fasted, prayed, laid hands on Barnabas and Saul and sent them out. In the next chapter of Acts they are referred to as apostles.

Acts 14:14 But when the apostles Barnabas and Paul heard this, they tore their clothes and ran in among the multitude, crying out ...

Life Completely Changed

Paul was completely changed. He had gone from zealously persecuting the Christians to becoming one himself. He had gone from being trained by man in the doctrines of man to being trained by God in the doctrines of God. He had gone from being hated and feared to being a leader of the body of Christ. He was a man chosen by God to reach the Gentile nations.

His life can be an encouragement to every one of us. His conversion can be an inspiration to others. No matter how deep in sin a person is, there is forgiveness in Jesus.

1 Timothy 1:15,16 This is a faithful saying and worthy of all accep-tance, that Christ Jesus came into the world to save sinners, of whom I am chief. However, for this reason I obtained mercy, that in me first Jesus Christ might show all longsuffering, as a pattern to those who are going to believe on Him for everlasting life.

QUESTIONS FOR REVIEW

1. Tell in your own words the background of the apostle Paul.

2. Give the definition of conversion.

3. How can the example of Paul's life, as you have studied it in this lesson, make a difference in your life?

Ministry and Death of Paul

WITH GREAT PERSECUTION

Paul was completely transformed when he had a personal encounter with Jesus Christ. His life is a study of trials, testings, persecutions, challenges and victories.

Man Made Blind
Acts 13:4-12

As soon as the church at Antioch had laid hands on Saul and Barnabas and sent them out, they went to the island of Cyprus. The Proconsul sent for them because he wanted to hear the Word of God. However, his attendant, Elymas, the sorcerer, opposed them.

Acts 13:8-12 But Elymas the sorcerer (for so his name is translated) withstood them, seeking to turn the proconsul away from the faith. Then Saul, who also is called Paul, filled with the Holy Spirit, looked intently at him and said, "O full of all deceit and all fraud, you son of the devil, you enemy of all righteousness, will you not cease perverting the straight ways of the Lord? And now, indeed, the hand of the Lord is upon you, and you shall be blind, not seeing the sun for a time."

And immediately a dark mist fell on him, and he went around seeking someone to lead him by the hand. Then the proconsul believed, when he saw what had been done, being astonished at the teaching of the Lord.

Paul walked in authority and used that authority to prevent the demon spirits in Elymas from turning the Proconsul away from faith in Jesus Christ.

Expelled From Region
Acts 13:14-52

When Paul and Barnabas came to Pisidian Antioch they were asked to speak in the synagogue if they had a word of encouragement. What more exciting word than that the Messiah had come? Paul stood and did a masterful job of preaching the gospel. He started with the people of Israel in Egypt, told of Moses, the prophets, David, John the Baptist, and the execution and resurrection of Jesus. Finally he told them that through Jesus they had forgiveness of their sins.

On the next Sabbath, almost the whole city gathered to hear the Word but the Jews were filled with jealousy and only the Gentiles heard and were glad.

The Jews incited the women of high standing and the leading men of the city and they expelled them from that region. As Paul and Barnabas left they shook the dust from their feet.

Paul Stoned, Left for Dead
Acts 14:1-20

Paul and Barnabas went on to Iconium and went to the synagogue. They spoke so effectively that a great number of Jews and Gentiles believed, but the unbelieving Jews stirred up the Gentiles and poisoned their minds.

Paul and Barnabas continued speaking boldly and their message was confirmed with signs and wonders, but the people of the city took sides. Soon there was a plot with both Jews and Gentiles against them with plans to stone them and they were forced once again to flee from the city.

Paul's experiences on his first missionary journey were really not ones that most of us would seek. In Lystra, a man was healed and the people tried to worship Paul and Barnabas. Jews came from Antioch and Iconium and incited the crowd. They stoned Paul and dragged him outside the city thinking he was dead. But after the disciples gathered around him, he got up.

Facing Reality

It is easy to read the accounts of the apostles and see only the exciting and wonderful parts. If we are to learn from them how Jesus wants His church built today, it is necessary that we see them as real people. They had their trials and testings just as we do. The reason they were victorious is that they never gave up!

We cannot be defeated if we just keep on doing what Jesus did. God can turn even our defeats into victories if we will let Him.

Actually in each of these cities people were saved. Miracles did happen. The name of Jesus was lifted up. But before we go on to study the miracles of Paul, it was necessary to point out some of the trials, testings and persecutions.

2 Corinthians 4:7-10 But we have this treasure in earthen vessels, that the excellence of the power may be of God and not of us. We are hard pressed on every side, yet not crushed; we are perplexed, but not in despair; persecuted, but not forsaken; struck down, but not destroyed– always carrying about in the body the dying of the Lord Jesus, that the life of Jesus also may be manifested in our body.

MIRACULOUS MINISTRY THROUGH THE HOLY SPIRIT

It is impossible here to study even all of the high points of the ministry of Paul. For the purpose of this course, to understand how the church of the living God is supposed to live and operate we will look at some of these incidents as examples of God's plan for us today.

Jesus did not speak of an early church and a later church. He said He would build "His church." The gifts of the Holy Spirit that He gave are needed by believers as much today as they were needed in the first century. God did not give the gifts of the Holy Spirit and reveal how they operated in spreading the gospel in the early church and then mysteriously, at some time, take those gifts back.

Anything that Peter, James and John did, anything that Paul did, anything that Jesus did, we are to do also. Jesus said that "the works that I do shall ye do also and greater works then these shall ye do."

Miraculous Leading

There is an interesting passage just before Paul had the vision and was called to the people of Macedonia. It says that they were kept from preaching the Word in the province of Asia.

Acts 16:6,7 Now when they had gone through Phrygia and the region of Galatia, they were forbidden by the Holy Spirit to preach the word in Asia. After they had come to Mysia, they tried to go into Bithynia, but the Spirit did not permit them.

We are not given any reason. We are just told that the Holy Spirit prevented them from going to these countries. It is just as necessary to hear God's voice when He says not to do something as it is to hear his voice when he says to do something.

It is important that we remember that Jesus did only what He saw the Father doing. We must learn to be sensitive to God's leading to do something – or not to do something. This is for our protection.

Miraculous Vision

God's revelation for His direction in their ministry came in a vision.

Acts 16:9-11 And a vision appeared to Paul in the night. A man of Macedonia stood and pleaded with him, saying, "Come over to Macedonia and help us."

Now after he had seen the vision, immediately we sought to go to Macedonia, concluding that the Lord had called us to preach the gospel to them. Therefore, sailing from Troas, we ran a straight course to Samothrace, and the next day came to Neapolis ...

They came to Philippi, a Roman colony and the leading city in Macedonia. There they met a woman named Lydia and she and members of her house were saved.

They were where God had sent them and there was an opportunity to minister. It was not a large congregation but a prayer group that met by the side of the river.

Miraculous Knowing

Paul and the others were on their way to a place of prayer when the girl began to follow them and cry out, "These men are servants of the Most High God, who are telling you the way to be saved." She continued shouting out this message for many days.

What she said was the truth. She was calling attention to them and would, perhaps, open doors for them to minister. But Paul was troubled in his spirit, and finally after many days he did something about it.

Acts 16:16-18 Now it happened, as we went to prayer, that a certain slave girl possessed with a spirit of divination met us, who brought her masters much profit by fortune-telling. This girl followed Paul and us, and cried out, saying, "These men are the servants of the Most High God, who proclaim to us the way of salvation." And this she did for many days.

But Paul, greatly annoyed, turned and said to the spirit, "I command you in the name of Jesus Christ to come out of her." And he came out that very hour.

Paul, through a supernatural gift of the Holy Spirit, recognized the spirit that was operating through this girl and he cast it out. This was the supernatural gift of "distinguishing between spirits" mentioned in First Corinthians thirteen.

Miraculous Release

The owners of the slave girl had Paul and Silas thrown into prison. They were stripped, beaten and put into the inner cell with their feet locked in stocks. But Paul and Silas were busy praying, singing hymns to God, and being witnesses to the other prisoners.

They were not spending their time saying, "God why did you tell us to come here?" They were not saying, "I guess we missed God's direction. He didn't tell us to come to Macedonia after all." Because they stayed in the Spirit, God could intervene in their behalf.

Acts 16:25-30 But at midnight Paul and Silas were praying and singing hymns to God, and the prisoners were listening to them. Suddenly there was a great earthquake, so that the foundations of the prison were shaken; and immediately all the doors were opened and everyone's chains were loosed. And the keeper of the prison, awaking from sleep and seeing the prison doors open, supposing the prisoners had fled, drew his sword and was about to kill himself.

But Paul called with a loud voice, saying, "Do yourself no harm, for we are all here."

Then he called for a light, ran in, and fell down trembling before Paul and Silas. And he brought them out and said, "Sirs, what must I do to be saved?"

God sent an earthquake to release Paul and Silas from the prison but the jailer and all his family were the ones truly set free.

The disciples left Philippi and traveled on to Thessalonica where again they taught and again opposition came. Their reputation was certainly going with them, because the men said "These men who have caused trouble all over the world have now come here ..."

Again they were forced to leave the city and Paul went on to Athens.

Miraculous Encouragement

➣ *Athens*

In Athens, Paul spent his time in the synagogues reasoning and arguing with the Jews. He was discussing doctrine and trying to persuade them that Jesus was the Messiah and some of them believed. The Jews became more and more abusive and finally Paul left the city. He had reason to be be discouraged.

Acts 18:4-6 And he reasoned in the synagogue every Sabbath, and persuaded both Jews and Greeks. When Silas and Timothy had come from Macedonia, Paul was constrained by the Spirit, and testified to the Jews that Jesus is the Christ. But when they opposed him and blasphemed, he shook his garments and said to them, "Your blood be upon your own heads; I am clean. From now on I will go to the Gentiles."

➣ *Corinth*

Paul went from Athens to Corinth and did the same things, and many did believe. God spoke to Paul again in a vision.

Acts 18:9,10 Now the Lord spoke to Paul in the night by a vision, "Do not be afraid, but speak, and do not keep silent; for I am with you, and no one will attack you to hurt you; for I have many people in this city."

This vision was a word of encouragement. "Right on Paul. You're doing great. Just keep on teaching and no one in this city is going to attack you!" Paul remained in Corinth for over a year and a half.

CHANGE IN METHODS

Ephesus

When Paul arrived in Ephesus his approach to ministry was different. He did not spend his time discussing doctrine and explaining the reasonableness of the gospel. He approached a group of believers and said "Did you receive the Holy Spirit when you believed?"

Acts 19:2-7 He said to them, "Did you receive the Holy Spirit when you believed?"

And they said to him, "We have not so much as heard whether there is a Holy Spirit."

And he said to them, "Into what then were you baptized?"

So they said, "Into John's baptism."

Then Paul said, "John indeed baptized with a baptism of repentance, saying to the people that they should believe on Him who would come after him, that is, on Christ Jesus."

When they heard this, they were baptized in the name of the Lord Jesus. And when Paul had laid hands on them, the Holy Spirit came upon them, and they spoke with tongues and prophesied. Now the men were about twelve in all.

Then Paul went into the synagogue and spoke boldly for three months and when the opposition started to get strong he left, but he did not leave the city.

Paul took the disciples to the lecture hall of Tyrannus and had discussions daily for two years. From this statement, it appears that Paul started a Bible School and multiplied himself into the lives of others.

The result was that all the Jews and Greeks who lived in the province of Asia heard the Word of the Lord.

Acts 19:8-10 And he went into the synagogue and spoke boldly for three months, reasoning and persuading concerning the things of the kingdom of God. But when some were hardened and did not believe, but spoke evil of the Way before the multitude, he departed from them and withdrew the disciples, reasoning daily in the school of Tyrannus. And this continued for two years, so that all who dwelt in Asia heard the word of the Lord Jesus, both Jews and Greeks.

God had prevented Paul from going into Asia before, but now all Asia heard the Word of the Lord. Perhaps God had wanted to change Paul's approach before He led him into Asia.

➤ *Brought Back from Death*

Paul was teaching at Troas and Eutychus was sitting in a window and he went to sleep and fell three stories and was killed.

Acts 20:7-11 Now on the first day of the week, when the disciples came together to break bread, Paul, ready to depart the next day, spoke to them and continued his message until midnight. There were many lamps in the upper room where they were gathered together. And in a window sat a certain young man named Eutychus, who was sinking into a deep sleep. He was overcome by sleep; and as Paul continued speaking, he fell down from the third story and was taken up dead.

But Paul went down, fell on him, and embracing him said, "Do not trouble yourselves, for his life is in him." Now when he had come up, had broken bread and eaten, and talked a long while, even till daybreak, he departed.

PAUL'S SUMMARY OF HIS MINISTRY

Paul was on his way back to Jerusalem and he was meeting with the elders of the Church of Ephesus for the last time. Paul summarized his ministry to this point.

Paul might have looked at his circumstances. He might have said, "God I gave up so much for you. I gave up a position of honor. I gave up a secure future. I am educated. I speak several languages. Yet, you ask me to minister to one man here and a few men there. I've been run out of every city you have sent me to. I have been beaten and left for dead. Lord, I'm tired and discouraged. I just want to give up and quit!"

Paul never engaged in any of that kind of talk!

Acts 20:19-24 ... serving the Lord with all humility, with many tears and trials which happened to me by the plotting of the Jews; and how I kept back nothing that was helpful, but proclaimed it to you, and taught you publicly and from house to house, testifying to Jews, and also to Greeks, repentance toward God and faith toward our Lord Jesus Christ. And see, now I go bound in the spirit to Jerusalem, not knowing the things that will happen to me there, except that the Holy Spirit testifies in every city, saying that chains and tribulations await me. But none of these things move me; nor do I count my life dear to myself, so that I may finish my race with joy, and the ministry which I received from the Lord Jesus, to testify to the gospel of the grace of God.

BOUND FOR JERUSALEM AND FOR ROME

Paul's Imprisonment Prophesied

As Paul was traveling to Jerusalem, he came to Caesarea and stayed at the home of the evangelist, Philip. While he was there, the prophet by the name of Agabus came.

Acts 21:10-11 And as we stayed many days, a certain prophet named Agabus came down from Judea. When he had come to us, he took Paul's belt, bound his own hands and feet, and said, "Thus says the Holy Spirit, 'So shall the Jews at Jerusalem bind the man who owns this belt, and deliver him into the hands of the Gentiles.' "

Paul's Arrest
Acts 21:1-23:22

It was the believers in Jerusalem that unwittingly led to Paul's arrest. They requested that he go through a purification rite and that would settle a problem among the Jews in Israel. Paul agreed and on the last day, the seventh day, he was in the temple when Jews from Asia saw him. These Jews assumed that Paul had brought Greek believers into the temple which was against the law and they began shouting.

Acts 21:30-36 And all the city was disturbed; and the people ran together, seized Paul, and dragged him out of the temple; and immediately the doors were shut. Now as they were seeking to kill him, news came to the commander of the garrison that all Jerusalem was in an uproar. He immediately took soldiers and centurions, and ran down to them. And when they saw the commander and the soldiers, they stopped beating Paul. Then the commander came near and took him, and commanded him to be bound with two chains; and he asked who he was and what he had done. And some among the multitude cried one thing and some another. And when he could not ascertain the truth because of the tumult, he commanded him to be taken into the barracks. And when he reached the stairs, he had to be carried by the soldiers because of the violence of the mob. For the multitude of the people followed after, crying out, "Away with him!"

Paul Witnessed to Mob

Paul spoke to the people from the top of the stairs but they would not believe. Again they began shouting.

Acts 22:22-24 And they listened to him until this word, and then they raised their voices and said, "Away with such a fellow from the earth, for he is not fit to live!" Then, as they cried out and tore off their clothes and threw dust into the air, the commander ordered him to be brought into the barracks, and said that he should be examined under scourging, so that he might know why they shouted so against him.

When they started to flog Paul he asked if it was legal for them to flog a Roman citizen that had not been found guilty.

Paul Witnessed to High Priest & Sanhedrin

The Roman commander realized that he could not hold Paul without legal charges and so he brought him before the chief priest and all the Sanhedrin. Through this situation Paul was allowed to witness concerning Jesus to all of the Sanhedrin.

The fight between factions of Sanhedrin became so fierce that the commander ordered his troops to take Paul away from them by force and bring him to the barracks.

Second Visit from Lord

Acts 23:11 But the following night the Lord stood by him and said, "Be of good cheer, Paul; for as you have testified for Me in Jerusalem, so you must also bear witness at Rome."

Paul was in prison, but his ministry was not over. By being a Roman he was given special favor in the prison and it actually became his protection while he witnessed wherever Jesus sent him.

IN CAESAREA

Military Protection
Acts 23:23-26:32

There was a plot to kill Paul by forty Jewish men. The commander ordered a detachment of two hundred soldiers, seventy horsemen, and two hundred spearmen to take Paul out of the city. Then the cavalry went on with him to the Roman Governor Felix in Caesarea that night.

Paul was imprisoned by Governor Felix but he had many opportunities to talk and witness to him and to his wife who was Jewish. Felix left Paul in prison for two years but he was given some freedom and his friends could come to see him.

Felix retired and Festus took his place as Governor. Festus at the instigation of the Jews brought Paul to court again and asked Paul if he would be willing to be tried in Jerusalem. Paul knew that he would never arrive alive in Jerusalem. He knew that the Lord had said he would testify of Him in Rome, so he appealed to Caesar. That was his right as a Roman citizen.

Paul Witnessed to Rulers

King Agrippa and Bernice and Governor Festus with the high ranking officers and the leading men of Caesarea were in the audience when Festus called for Paul to come. What an opportunity! Paul again told them about the light on the road to Damascus, about his conversion, and about the resurrected Jesus.

Acts 26:28,29 Then Agrippa said to Paul, "You almost persuade me to become a Christian."

And Paul said, "I would to God that not only you, but also all who hear me today, might become both almost and altogether such as I am, except for these chains."

Paul's goal was the same in prison or out – to win the world to Jesus. That should be our one goal also.

PAUL SAILS FOR ROME

Victory in Face of Disaster
Acts 27

Paul was put in the charge of a centurion by the name of Julius and sent to Rome by ship. Travel then was almost impossible for us to imagine. They would stop at a port for a week, a month, a winter. Even in the best of conditions the trip to Rome would take several weeks.

➤ *Paul Gave Warning*

When they stopped at Crete, Paul warned them because of a word of wisdom not to continue on.

Acts 27:10,11 Saying, "Men, I perceive that this voyage will end with disaster and much loss, not only of the cargo and ship, but also our lives." Nevertheless the centurion was more persuaded by the helmsman and the owner of the ship than by the things spoken by Paul.

Just as Paul had said, they were caught in a terrible storm. They put ropes around the ship trying to hold it together. They threw the cargo and the tackle overboard. When the storm continued raging for many days, they gave up all hope of living.

➤ *Prophesied "Not One to be Lost"*

Acts 27:21-26 But after long abstinence from food, then Paul stood in the midst of them and said, "Men, you should have listened to me, and not have sailed from Crete and incurred this disaster and loss. And now I urge you to take heart, for there will be no loss of life among you, but only of the ship.

For there stood by me this night an angel of the God to whom I belong and whom I serve, saying, 'Do not be afraid, Paul; you must be brought before Caesar; and indeed God has granted you all those who sail with you.' Therefore take heart, men, for I believe God that it will be just as it was told me. However, we must run aground on a certain island."

The crew tried to escape in a lifeboat but Paul went to the centurion. This time he listened to Paul. The soldiers cut the ropes to the life boat and kept the sailors on the ship as Paul had said.

> *Witnessed to Soldiers, Crew*

Acts 27:33-37 And as day was about to dawn, Paul implored them all to take food, saying, "Today is the fourteenth day you have waited and continued without food, and eaten nothing. Therefore I urge you to take nourishment, for this is for your survival, since not a hair will fall from the head of any of you." And when he had said these things, he took bread and gave thanks to God in the presence of them all; and when he had broken it he began to eat. Then they were all encouraged, and also took food themselves. And in all we were two hundred and seventy-six persons on the ship.

Acts 27:41-44 But striking a place where two seas met, they ran the ship aground; and the prow stuck fast and remained immovable, but the stern was being broken up by the violence of the waves.

> *Everyone Was Saved*

Now the soldiers' plan was to kill the prisoners, lest any of them should swim away and escape. But the centurion, wanting to save Paul, kept them from their purpose, and commanded that those who could swim should jump overboard first and get to land, and the rest, some on boards and some on broken pieces of the ship. And so it was that they all escaped safely to land.

ISLAND OF MALTA

Acts 28:1-10
Viper Attack

They were stranded on the island of Malta and the island people built a fire to help them dry out and get warm and Paul had gathered a pile of brushwood.

Acts 28:3-6 But when Paul had gathered a bundle of sticks and laid them on the fire, a viper came out because of the heat, and fastened on his hand. So when the natives saw the creature hanging from his hand, they said to one another, "No doubt this man is a murderer, whom, though he has escaped the sea, yet justice does not allow to live."

But he shook off the creature into the fire and suffered no harm. However, they were expecting that he would swell up or suddenly fall down dead; but after they had looked for a long time and saw no harm come to him, they changed their minds and said that he was a god.

Jesus had said that there was a sign that would follow believers. They could pick up serpents. Jesus gave His divine protection to all of those who would believe in His name.

Paul Witnesses to Publius

The chief official of Malta was Publius. His father was sick and even though Luke, the doctor, was there, it was Paul that healed him.

Acts 28:8,9 And it happened that the father of Publius lay sick of a fever and dysentery. Paul went in to him and prayed, and he laid his

hands on him and healed him. So when this was done, the rest of those on the island who had diseases also came and were healed.

PAUL WITNESSED IN ROME

Acts 28:15-31

Paul's status had certainly changed on the trip to Rome. He was still a prisoner but he was given some freedom.

Welcoming Committee

The believers had heard that Paul and Luke were coming to Rome and they came to meet them.

Acts 28:15 And from there, when the brethren heard about us, they came to meet us as far as Appii Forum and Three Inns. When Paul saw them, he thanked God and took courage.

Paul's Witness to Jews

Acts 28:23-25 So when they had appointed him a day, many came to him at his lodging, to whom he explained and solemnly testified of the kingdom of God, persuading them concerning Jesus from both the Law of Moses and the Prophets, from morning till evening. And some were persuaded by the things which were spoken, and some disbelieved. So when they did not agree among themselves, they departed after Paul had said one word: "The Holy Spirit spoke rightly through Isaiah the prophet to our fathers ..."

Paul's Witness to Gentiles

Act 28:28,29 "Therefore let it be known to you that the salvation of God has been sent to the Gentiles, and they will hear it!" And when he had said these words, the Jews departed and had a great dispute among themselves.

Book of Acts Ends

Acts 28:30-31 Then Paul dwelt two whole years in his own rented house, and received all who came to him, preaching the kingdom of God and teaching the things which concern the Lord Jesus Christ with all confidence, no one forbidding him.

Death of Paul

According to tradition Paul was beheaded in Rome. His Roman citizenship allowed him the "privilege" of being beheaded rather than crucified.

Summary

Book after book of the New Testament is written by the apostle Paul. What an example he is of God's grace.

He is an example of a believer who allows absolutely nothing to intervene between himself and obedience to God. He took the message of Jesus into the synagogue. He reasoned, argued, taught, and rebuked when necessary. He had made a decision that nothing would ever stop him from doing the will of the Father, not even the fear of death. **God is still looking for fearless Pauls today!**

QUESTIONS FOR REVIEW

1. Describe in your own words some of the incidents of Paul's first missionary trip and how you can relate to it.

2. Give one example of supernatural leading in the life of Paul.

3. Why did Paul insist in going to Jerusalem even though he knew what would happen?

We Are the Church Triumphant

GOD'S PLAN HAS NEVER CHANGED

Just as the early disciples, apostles, prophets, pastors, teachers and evangelists operated in the first years of the church they are to operate today.

Just as the believers operated in that day, they are to operate today.

Just as wonders and miraculous signs were the stimulus for the growth of the beginning church they are to be today.

The Great Commission given to the first believers by Jesus has never been canceled. Jesus said,

Mark 16:15-20 And He said to them, "Go into all the world and preach the gospel to every creature. He who believes and is baptized will be saved; but he who does not believe will be condemned. And these signs will follow those who believe: In My name they will cast out demons; they will speak with new tongues; they will take up serpents; and if they drink anything deadly, it will by no means hurt them; they will lay hands on the sick, and they will recover." So then, after the Lord had spoken to them, He was received up into heaven, and sat down at the right hand of God. And they went out and preached everywhere, the Lord working with them and confirming the word through the accompanying signs. Amen.

HOW DID THE BEGINNING CHURCH OPERATE?

With Total Commitment

We have studied the lives of several of the church leaders. We have seen their total commitment even to the point of death. Sometimes, it might seem easier to die for our faith than to live in the hassles of this world, but total commitment will put those trials in proper perspective.

Philippians 3:13 Brethren, I do not count myself to have apprehended; but one thing I do, forgetting those things which are behind and reaching forward to those things which are ahead ...

Hebrews 12:1,2 Therefore we also, since we are surrounded by so great a cloud of witnesses, let us lay aside every weight, and the sin which so easily ensnares us, and let us run with endurance the race that is set before us, looking unto Jesus, the author and finisher of our faith, who for the joy that was set before Him endured the cross, despising the shame, and has sat down at the right hand of the throne of God.

Philippians 1:21 For to me, to live is Christ, and to die is gain.

When our only goal is Jesus and we really believe that to die is gain, there will be nothing in this world or in the spirit world that can stop us.

In Forgiveness

➤ *Jesus Chose to Forgive*

As Jesus was dying on the cross, He forgave all mankind. He forgave the religious Jews who had plotted His death. He forgave Pilate. He forgave the soldiers. He forgave the masses of people that had cried for His crucifixion. Jesus forgave the very beings that He had created, for rejecting Him and putting Him to death. What has happened to us that is worse than that?

Forgiveness is an act of our will. Just as Jesus forgave, we can choose to forgive.

Unless we think that Jesus could only forgive because he was God and man in one being, we are told how Stephen also forgave as they were killing him. He too, in the last moments of death cried, "Lord, do not hold this sin against them."

➤ *Stephen Chose to Forgive*

If Stephen had been bitter and railing, "God how could you let them do this to me?" If he had been speaking curses on them instead of asking God for their forgiveness, would his face have been radiant? Would he have been allowed to see Jesus standing at the right hand of the Father? Would Saul, standing there agreeing with the others in his death, have been impressed?

➤ *We Must Forgive*

It is necessary that we forgive so that we can be forgiven!

Matthew 6:14,15 For if you forgive men their trespasses, your heavenly Father will also forgive you. But if you do not forgive men their trespasses, neither will your Father forgive your trespasses.

Ephesians 4:31,32 Let all bitterness, wrath, anger, clamor, and evil speaking be put away from you, with all malice. And be kind to one another, tenderhearted, forgiving one another, just as God in Christ also forgave you.

In Submission

The believers of the beginning church were in submission one to another and all to Jesus. They were also in submission to the governments over them.

1 Peter 2:13-20 Therefore submit yourselves to every ordinance of man for the Lord's sake, whether to the king as supreme, or to governors, as to those who are sent by him for the punishment of evildoers and for the praise of those who do good. For this is the will of God, that by doing good you may put to silence the ignorance of foolish men—as free, yet not using your liberty as a cloak for vice, but as servants of God.

Honor all people. Love the brotherhood. Fear God. Honor the king. Servants, be submissive to your masters with all fear, not only to the good and gentle, but also to the harsh. For this is commendable, if because of conscience toward God one endures grief, suffering wrongfully. For what credit is it if, when you are beaten for your faults, you take it patiently? But when you do good and suffer for it, if you take it patiently, this is commendable before God.

In Obedience

Jesus said that we show our love for Him by being obedient to Him. Sometimes we pray, "Lord show me what you want me to do and I will do it!" But we are not praying in total honesty. God has shown us through His Word what we are to do. To be obedient we must first do these things on a daily basis and then trust God to show us any particular tasks He has for us to do. As we walk in obedience these other things will be known to us.

John 14:15,21 If you love Me, keep My commandments. He who has My commandments and keeps them, it is he who loves Me. And he who loves Me will be loved by My Father, and I will love him and manifest Myself to him.

1 John 2:3-6 Now by this we know that we know Him, if we keep His commandments. He who says, "I know Him," and does not keep His commandments, is a liar, and the truth is not in him. But whoever keeps His word, truly the love of God is perfected in him. By this we know that we are in Him. He who says he abides in Him ought himself also to walk just as He walked.

What are his commandments?

➢ That we receive His Holy Spirit
➢ That we be baptized in water
➢ That we forgive one another
➢ That we love one another
➢ That we come together in fellowship
➢ That we give tithes and offerings
➢ That we tell others about the resurrected Christ
➢ That we study His Word
➢ That we walk in integrity

With Unity

Being in unity does not mean there will never be any disagreements between us. It means that we will handle those disagreements in love, come to an agreement, forgive anything and everything that has been said out of the Spirit, and go on together to win this world to Jesus.

To study how to handle disagreements in doctrine we have an example in Acts fifteen on the subject of whether every believer had to be circumcised.

Jesus gave us definite instruction on how to handle personal disagreements, or sin in the life of another believer.

Matthew 18:15-17 Moreover if your brother sins against you, go and tell him his fault between you and him alone. If he hears you, you have gained your brother. But if he will not hear you, take with you one or two more, that 'by the mouth of two or three witnesses every word may be established.' And if he refuses to hear them, tell it to the church. But if he refuses even to hear the church, let him be to you like a heathen and a tax collector.

There are three steps to take when there is something between us and a fellow believer.

> First, we are to go directly to him and talk it over.
> If it is not resolved, we are to take one or two others with us and go back to that brother.
> Finally, if he refuses to listen we are to take the situation to the church and if he refuses to listen even then, we are to stay away from him.

Colossians 3:16 Let the word of Christ dwell in you richly in all wisdom, teaching and admonishing one another in psalms and hymns and spiritual songs, singing with grace in your hearts to the Lord.

Philippians 1:27 Only let your conduct be worthy of the gospel of Christ, so that whether I come and see you or am absent, I may hear of your affairs, that you stand fast in one spirit, with one mind striving together for the faith of the gospel ...

Philippians 2:2 And not in any way terrified by your adversaries, which is to them a proof of perdition, but to you of salvation, and that from God.

GOD HAS GIVEN US HIS POWER

Jesus instructed the disciples to wait in Jerusalem until they had received power.

Acts 1:8 But you shall receive power when the Holy Spirit has come upon you; and you shall be witnesses to Me in Jerusalem, and in all Judea and Samaria, and to the end of the earth.

According to Paul that power included the following:

> the message of wisdom
> the message of knowledge
> faith
> gifts of healing
> miraculous power
> prophecy
> distinguishing between spirits
> speaking in different kinds of tongues
> the interpretation of tongues

We call these the gifts, or messages, of the Holy Spirit.

I Corinthians 12:8-11 For to one is given the word of wisdom through the Spirit, to another the word of knowledge through the same Spirit, to another faith by the same Spirit, to another gifts of healings by the same Spirit, to another the working of miracles, to another prophecy, to another discerning of spirits, to another different kinds of tongues, to another the interpretation of tongues. But one and the same Spirit works all these things, distributing to each one individually as He wills.

If we have the infilling of the Holy Spirit, we have all of His gifts operating through us as they are needed for the common good.

I Corinthians 12:4-7 Now there are diversities of gifts, but the same Spirit. There are differences of ministries, but the same Lord. And there are diversities of activities, but it is the same God who works all in all. But the manifestation of the Spirit is given to each one for the profit of all ...

GOD HAS GIVEN US HIS NAME

To become a Christian we must believe that Jesus is the Son of God, that He was born of a virgin and had no sin, that He died on the cross as a sacrifice for our sins, that He conquered death and the grave and lives today at the right hand of the Father.

To operate in power as a Christian we must believe in the power of His name. His name is the only authority we have in which to operate on this earth. We are told to do all in the name of Jesus!

Colossians 3:17 And whatever you do in word or deed, do all in the name of the Lord Jesus, giving thanks to God the Father through Him.

What is the Great Commission? A commandment of things to do in the name of Jesus.

Mark 16:17b,18 In My name they will cast out demons; they will speak with new tongues; they will take up serpents; and if they drink anything deadly, it will by no means hurt them; they will lay hands on the sick, and they will recover.

WHERE DO WE START?

Where We Are

Jesus told the disciples that they would minister first in Jerusalem and then reach out to other areas of the world.

Acts 1:8 But you shall receive power when the Holy Spirit has come upon you; and you shall be witnesses to Me in Jerusalem, and in all Judea and Samaria, and to the end of the earth.

Commitment to Church

Using Paul as an example, we notice that he first told of Jesus in Damascus where he was converted. He taught in the synagogue but he stayed with the disciples. Then Paul was in a period of silent time – just him and the Lord. During this time he was not ministering to others.

Then Paul went to Jerusalem and met some of the apostles and spent some time with them and they sent him on to Tarsus. Barnabas came after Paul and took him back to the church in Antioch. After his first missionary trip, Paul returned to the church in Antioch.

Acts 14:26-28 From there they sailed to Antioch, where they had been commended to the grace of God for the work which they had completed. And when they had come and gathered the church together, they reported all that God had done with them, and that

He had opened the door of faith to the Gentiles. So they stayed there a long time with the disciples.

Paul also was in contact with the apostles in Jerusalem and returned there often.

All of the apostles were in contact with one another. They had differences of opinions but they worked them out and stayed in unity with one purpose and that was to strengthen the body and to win the world to Jesus Christ.

QUESTIONS THAT SHOULD BE ANSWERED

Fellowship

✥ **Are you faithful in coming together with others in the body of Christ?**

1 John 1:3,7 That which we have seen and heard we declare to you, that you also may have fellowship with us; and truly our fellowship is with the Father and with His Son Jesus Christ. But if we walk in the light as He is in the light, we have fellowship with one another, and the blood of Jesus Christ His Son cleanses us from all sin.

Ephesians 2:19-22 Now, therefore, you are no longer strangers and foreigners, but fellow citizens with the saints and members of the household of God, having been built on the foundation of the apostles and prophets, Jesus Christ Himself being the chief cornerstone, in whom the whole building, being joined together, grows into a holy temple in the Lord, in whom you also are being built together for a habitation of God in the Spirit.

Hebrews 10:24,25 And let us consider one another in order to stir up love and good works, not forsaking the assembling of ourselves together, as is the manner of some, but exhorting one another, and so much the more as you see the Day approaching.

Tithes and Offerings

✥ **Are you faithful in giving your tithes and offerings?**

Many believers find that money is one of the hardest areas to totally commit to God. We want to serve God, but we want to control our own money. There are many, many verses on the subject of money, but we will use only one passage because it makes it clear that we are to give both tithes and offerings. An offering is an amount above our tithe.

God wants us to tithe and give offerings so that He can bless us. He cannot go against His Word and bless us before we obey Him.

Some have said, "I have needs and after they are met I will begin to tithe." Some have said " I will give tithes to Him when I have more income." God's Word is very specific and every believer is to tithe and give offerings.

Malachi 3:8-12 "Will a man rob God? Yet you have robbed Me! But you say, 'In what way have we robbed You?' In tithes and offerings. You are cursed with a curse, for you have robbed Me, even this whole nation. Bring all the tithes into the storehouse, that there may be food in My house, and prove Me now in this," says the LORD of hosts, "If I will not open for you the windows of heaven And pour out for you such blessing that there will not be room enough to receive it. And I will rebuke the devourer for your sakes, so that he will not destroy the fruit of your ground, nor shall the vine fail to bear fruit for you in the field," says the LORD of hosts; "and all nations will call you blessed, for you will be a delightful land," says the LORD of hosts.

Because believers today have not been taught the necessity of tithing to be obedient to God, they are under a curse. God challenges us to test Him in this one area, to bring our tithe to his storehouse and see if He will not throw open the windows of heaven to pour out blessings on us.

The Hebrew word used as "storehouse" here means the armory, the place where the weapons are stored. It was a place where the power was stored. Today, we are to give our tithes and offerings to local churches and to ministries of power.

Your Reputation

↳ Could a local church recommend you?

Acts 9:27 But Barnabas took him and brought him to the apostles. And he declared to them how he had seen the Lord on the road, and that He had spoken to him, and how he had preached boldly at Damascus in the name of Jesus.

↳ Has your responsibility, and integrity and faithfulness been recognized by the elders of your church?

Faithfulness includes having a serving attitude, being there when needed, giving your tithe, and being involved in study of the Word.

Study of Word

↳ Are you willing to invest time to study and learn?

2 Timothy 2:15 Be diligent to present yourself approved to God, a worker who does not need to be ashamed, rightly dividing the word of truth.

To "tell" the Good News, first you must "know" the truths of God's Word.

QUESTIONS FOR REVIEW

1. Name five aspects of how the church operated in the beginnning.

2. Why did Jesus instruct His first disciples to wait in Jerusalem?

3. Could a local church recommend you? Why, or why not?

THERE IS NO CONCLUSION!

There is no way that we can ever finish the study of the Triumphant Church of Jesus Christ. The New Testament from the book of Acts to Jude is the story of its beginning. The book of Revelation is still the prophecy of its final hours.

God's plan has never changed.

The church that began at the day of Pentecost
and grew through the ministry of Peter and the other apostles,
is still growing today.

The church that suffered with Stephen
and the other martyrs that followed him,
is still suffering with its martyrs today.

The church that grew through wonders and miraculous signs
confirming who Jesus was,
is still growing through signs and wonders today.

The church that did the works that Jesus did,
is still doing His works today.

Nations have come and gone but the church of Jesus Christ
is still very much alive and growing.

It is a living, vital being made up
of the living, committed believers of today.

As Jesus said,
"I will build my church and the gates of hell
shall not prevail against it."